Ancient Peoples and Places

THE ESKIMOS AND ALEUTS

General Editor

PROFESSOR GLYN DANIEL

ABOUT THE AUTHOR

Don E. Dumond was born in 1929 and brought up on a ranch in northern New Mexico, later going on to study English literature at the University of New Mexico. After four years' military service mainly in Korea and Japan, he moved to Mexico, where in 1957 he received an MA degree in Latin American studies. His interest in the problems of Eskaleut archaeology was fostered at the University of Oregon, where he took his doctorate in 1962, and became successively Assistant Professor, Associate Professor and Professor of Anthropology, which latter position he still holds. In the past two decades he has carried out seasons of fieldwork and excavation in Alaska, as well as research trips to Mexico, and has published numerous articles on Arctic prehistory in learned journals.

THE ESKIMOS AND ALEUTS

Don E. Dumond

WITH 119 ILLUSTRATIONS

THAMES AND HUDSON

For Mary and Lester, who made it possible

THIS IS VOLUME EIGHTY-SEVEN IN THE SERIES
Ancient Peoples and Places
GENERAL EDITOR: PROFESSOR GLYN DANIEL

Maps and line drawings by Carol Steichen Dumond

First published in 1977 by Thames and Hudson Ltd, London

Filmset in Great Britain by Keyspools Ltd, Golborne, Lancashire and printed in Great Britain by BAS Printers Ltd, Over Wallop, Hampshire

CONTENTS

Preface

The Eskimos, and the adventures of Europeans in Eskimo country, have been a favourite topic in western literature for more than a century. This interest – no doubt stimulated by admiration for the Eskimos' effective adaptation to a particularly inhospitable region – has in the past been focused upon that great area above the Arctic Circle and between Point Barrow in Alaska on the west and Thule in Greenland on the east. The native people whom one meets in the multitudinous accounts are rarely the folk of southern Greenland or of the Alaskan coast south of Point Hope, who collectively greatly outnumber their northern kin of the true Arctic. Least of all has interest been shown in the Eskimo-speaking peoples of the southern Bering Sea and north Pacific Ocean, and in their linguistic cousins the Aleuts, scattered from the Alaska Peninsula through the Aleutian chain of islands. The few works that deal with the prehistory of Eskimos suffer a similar bias, ignoring or at least displaying a basic unfamiliarity with the importance of these western southerners in the development of the Eskimo way of life.

Yet it is precisely in this area between Bering Strait on the north and the Aleutian Islands and Alaska Peninsula on the south that the majority of the Eskimo-Aleut or Eskaleut people live. And it is here that most of the crucial intellectual advances of Eskimo prehistory were made, developments which led ultimately to the complete domination of the northernmost American coastline for a combined distance of 11,000 kilometres by people of a surprisingly homogeneous culture.

One aim of this book is partially to redress the balance by presenting the prehistory of the Eskaleut peoples from the centre of gravity of both their population distribution and their prehistoric identity. As the story develops, however, and despite the fact that both Eskimos and Aleuts are clearly and thoroughly American, it will become clear that the prehistory of these most Asiatic of native Americans cannot be fully understood without a comparable understanding of the prehistory of the Asian coasts of the Bering and Chukchi Seas and of far-eastern Siberia. Unfortunately, knowledge of these Asian areas lags behind that of the Alaskan landmass – sketchily as even this is known – so that all that will be possible here is to point to those aspects of Siberian prehistory which now seem most significant.

Unlike Mexico and areas of the Old World where locally developed calendrical systems are correlated with the Christian calendar with at least moderate success, chronology in northern North America is founded almost entirely upon age estimates by radioactive carbon. And since this radiocarbon time-scale, based upon the originally projected 5568-year half-life of carbon-14, is employed so consistently in the Arctic archaeological literature, it will be used exclusively in this book, with no attempt to convert dates to the Christian calendar by means of corrections recently introduced from dendrochronological studies of the bristlecone pine. Uncorrected dates for the pre-Christian era will be designated in lower-case letters (for example, 965 bc), following current convention. Those who may feel an occasional need to relate radiocarbon time to 'real' time, however, should find the following information helpful.

For present purposes, radiocarbon dates within the Christian era are accurate enough for variations to be ignored. Radiocarbon dates between 6500 and 3000 bc can be corrected roughly by placing them about 830 years earlier. There is no correction information for dates before 6500 bc. For the radiocarbon time between 3000 bc and the beginning of the Christian era, the following approximations apply:

C-14 date	Calendar date
500 bc	600 B C
1000	1200
1500	1900
2000	2500
2500	3200
3000	3800

I believe that the reconstruction of the bare outlines of Eskaleut prehistory presented in the following pages will be acceptable to most of my colleagues working in the north. Where significant disagreements exist I have been at pains to so indicate either in the text or in the brief notes that accompany some of the bibliographies. I have tried to limit my use of unpublished material to those works which I have definite permission to draw upon, or to those that have already been circulated so widely and quoted so often that there can be no further question of permission. Thinking of the non-specialist reader, however, I have refrained from listing any works in the bibliography that are not available through normal library channels.

The background for this book began to be accumulated, willy-nilly, seventeen years ago when the University of Oregon began sustained research in south-western Alaska. At that time, a conspiracy between George Y. Harry – of what was then the Bureau of Commercial Fisheries of the US Fish and Wildlife Service, who hoped that archaeology could tell him something of the long-term history of Alaskan salmon behaviour – and Luther S. Cressman – then chairman of the Department of Anthropology at the University of Oregon – sent me unexpectedly to the Sub-arctic to devise archaeology between clouds of insects, straying Alaska Brown bears, soaking rains and frozen soil. Ten field seasons later, in spite of everything, I am honestly grateful to them. I also extend my thanks to the various US government agencies and to the foundations, public and private, which made financially possible those ten summers and the never-ending analysis that has come from them – the National Science Foundation, the National Park Service, the National Geographic Society, the National Marine Fisheries Service (formerly the Bureau of Commercial Fisheries) and the Social Science Research Council.

As fate would arrange it, this period of research has spanned the time of the passage and implementation of the Alaska Native Claims Settlement Act of 1971, whereby a large amount of land in Alaska – once federal Public Lands – is being ceded to Alaskan natives (those legally identified as Eskimos, Aleuts and Indians) and to the State of Alaska. I am especially grateful to the people of these newly incorporated villages of the Alaska Peninsula, who have not only consistently provided moral and material support as individuals, but who in their new collectivity have so generously given permission to excavate on their lands – and whose story this book attempts to present in barest outline.

Closer to home, I must again mention the University of Oregon, which has unfailingly furnished both material and intellectual means for continuing research, and has attracted that lengthening progression of students, graduate and undergraduate, who have contributed the muscle to move the earth and the stamina to face often difficult living conditions. In this connection, I should like to mention in particular Harvey S. Rice, Michael Nowak, Gerald H. Clark and Winfield Henn, who have undertaken various aspects of laboratory analysis of the materials.

Ten field seasons spent almost exclusively in one small section of the Alaska Peninsula can easily make that spot seem the very navel of the universe. It is my colleagues, the small handful of professional archaeologists working in the Arctic, who are responsible for having made whatever dents are present in my own provincial armour. I salute and thank them all. Some of them, as well as the various universities and museums with which they are affiliated, are listed specifically in the photographic credits.

Most of all, I have pride in expressing my indebtedness to Carol Steichen Dumond, my wife, for her consistent interest through years of research, for her careful editorial eye, and for her maps and drawings.

CHAPTER I

Discovery : Search for New Worlds

The first direct encounters between Europeans and the various peoples described in this book began with no single dramatic sequence of events, but rather were spread across nearly 1000 years and 11,000 kilometres, and were parts of diverse episodes in the history of western expansion.

THE NORSE

In the later ninth century A D, emigrating Norsemen began to move into islands of the north-east Atlantic – Ireland, the Hebrides, the Shetlands, Orkneys, Faroes and, farther west still, Iceland. Sometime before 930 Greenland or its outlying rocky islets had been sighted, but no landing was made. Then in 982 Eric the Red, an Icelander, was banished for three years from his native land and went to spend them in south-western Greenland.

Greenland is a strange country, an island nearly large enough to be a continent, three-quarters of it above the Arctic Circle, its habitable areas a doughnut of mountainous tundra surrounding a mile-thick block of ice. But Eric found sea mammals along the coast and pasture in the tundra, and in 986 he returned to colonize. Two centres were established – the East Settlement in today's Julianehaab district, the West in the region of Godthaab. There were apparently no native inhabitants in these locations, although an account written nearly 140 years later reported that 'both east and west in the country they came across traces of people who had lived there, and bits of skin boats and stone implements'. Subsequent coastal hunting for fish and sea mammals undoubtedly brought Norsemen into direct contact with Eskimos in northern Greenland – and so Europeans saw their first Americans.

Shortly after A D 1000 Eric's son Leif sailed still farther westwards, finding lands he called Helluland, Markland, and Vinland. The identification of these is disputed, but they are most often said to be Baffinland, Labrador and northern Newfoundland. Leif passed a winter in Vinland, and according to one saga his trip was shortly repeated by his brother Thorvaldr, whose party spent three years in the place, although Thorvaldr himself was killed after two winters in a fight with 'Skraelings', as the Norse called the natives. Subsequent settlements were attempted by various of Leif's relatives, but other fights with Skraelings led to Norse withdrawal. Whether these natives were Eskimos or Indians is not clear; nevertheless, the Norse must have seen traces of Eskimos along the coasts of Labrador and Baffinland.

Although the urge to colonize the west died out, there are hints that the early Norse of treeless Greenland came to make regular trips to the Labrador woods for timber to build boats. If this is true, the Labrador Eskimos would certainly have made themselves known. In any event, by A D 1200 the settlements of Eskimos in north-west Greenland contained items of Norse manufacture, indicating a measure of trade within Greenland itself.

Throughout the thirteenth century the Norse colony prospered, but by the middle of the following century their situation had deteriorated: 'Now', it was reported, 'the Skraelings have the entire West Settlement; but there are horses, goats, cows and sheep, all wild'.

In another fifty years, contact with Europe flagged. For reasons of European politics and worsening climate, no Scandinavian ships went to Greenland after 1410, and hostilities with infiltrating Eskimos seem to have increased. By the end of the fifteenth century, the East Settlement too was made desolate – perhaps by raiding Eskimos, perhaps by maurauding English or Basque seamen. In any event, by the time of a visit by Icelanders in 1540 there were no Norse settlements or Norsemen to be seen, and by this time Eskimos occupied or regularly traversed the entire coasts of both east and west Greenland.

Although Greenland Eskimos were visited for trade in the late seventeenth century, the island was not reoccupied by Scandinavians until 1721 – this time by the Danes. Shortly thereafter knowledge of the Greenland Eskimos spread throughout Europe.

THE ENGLISH

The first flicker of British interest in a sea route westwards to the Orient was signalled by the voyages in 1497 and 1498 by John Cabot. Although his indeterminate results did nothing to stimulate lasting official interest in the Northwest Passage, the next century saw British, as well as Basque and French, fishermen and whalers successfully exploiting Canadian waters. Newfoundland was their American base, but there are no records of contact with natives.

Interest in the Passage to riches revived in 1576 when Martin Frobisher set out with two small ships, skirted the coast of Greenland, and reached Baffinland at Frobisher Bay, which he took to be the Passage. Landing, he encountered 'men in small boates made of leather', traded some trifles with them, and saw them capture five of his men. Seeking a hostage for their release, he lured one native to the side of his ship, seized him and 'plucked him with maine force boate and al into his bark out of the sea'. The captive Englishmen were not returned, however, and the hostage was hauled away to England, shortly to die of a respiratory disorder.

Because a rock he had found was said to contain gold, Frobisher was appointed general of a second expedition, returning to Frobisher Bay in 1577. Efforts on the part of the loyal general to locate and free his five

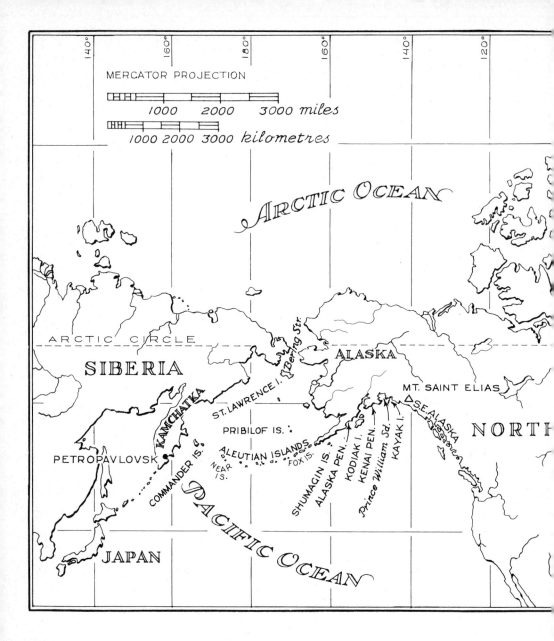

MERCATOR PROJECTION

1000 2000 3000 *miles*

1000 2000 3000 *kilometres*

ARCTIC OCEAN

ARCTIC CIRCLE

SIBERIA

ALASKA

MT. SAINT ELIAS

NORTH

KAMCHATKA

ST. LAWRENCE I.

Bering Str.

PRIBILOF IS.

ALEUTIAN ISLANDS

FOX IS.

S.E. ALASKA

KODIAK I.

KENAI PEN.

KAYAK I.

PETROPAVLOVSK

COMMANDER IS.

NEAR IS.

SHUMAGIN IS.

ALASKA PEN.

Prince William Sd.

PACIFIC OCEAN

JAPAN

1   The northern North American focus of European expansion, AD 900–1900.

2

captive seamen resulted in some abortive skirmishes, in one of which a pair of counter-attacking natives 'hurte the generall in the buttocke with an arrow, who then rather speedily fled backe', but he succeeded in capturing a native man, a woman, and her child. With Frobisher this year was John White, who produced at least four watercolours of the Eskimo captives and of the fighting. The captives were carried to England and, again, to early deaths from sickness.

The 'ore' brought back on the second expedition led to a third and grander one in 1578, when fifteen ships left England not only to mine and explore, but to leave a permanent colony. After a hard and uncomfortable summer, in which one ship sank, but in which Frobisher

GREENLAND

ICELAND

● GODTHAAB
(WEST SETTLEMENT)
● JULIANEHAAB
(EAST SETTLEMENT)

BAFFINLAND

Hudson Strait
Frobisher Bay

HUDSON
BAY

LABRADOR

AMERICA

NEWFOUNDLAND

EUROPE

ATLANTIC OCEAN

discovered and entered Hudson Strait, the plan to colonize was abandoned, and all surviving ships returned to England laden with 'ore', only to discover that it was worthless. Thus ended Frobisher's American adventure.

But English explorations continued between Greenland and Baffinland. In 1610 Henry Hudson sailed up Hudson Strait to Hudson Bay, then south to its south-eastern extension, where his ship was frozen in. When the ice broke up the following spring, the mutinous crew put Hudson, his son, two loyal seamen and five sick into a small boat and cast them adrift, never to be heard from again. Eskimos killed four of the mutineers near Hudson Strait; nine survivors returned home.

(Overleaf)
2 Eskimo man and woman (with her child in her parka hood) captured by Frobisher at Frobisher Bay in 1577. Watercolour drawings by John White.

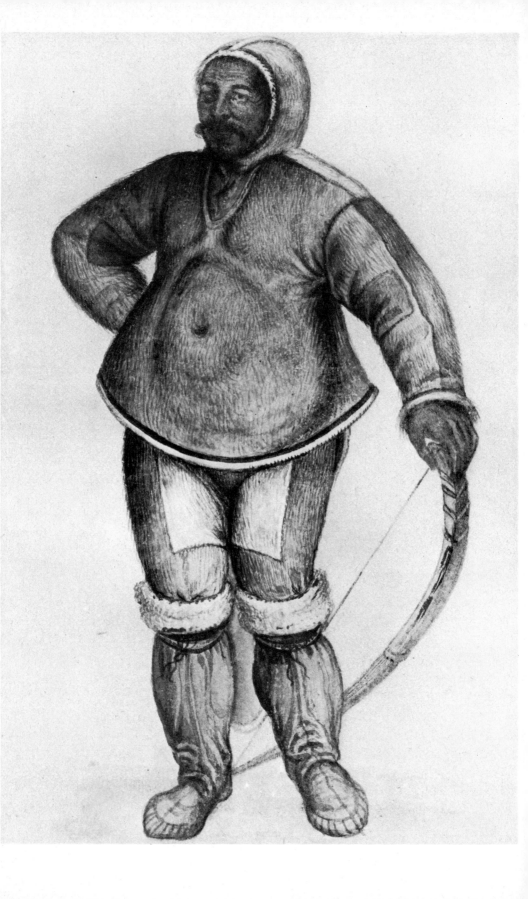

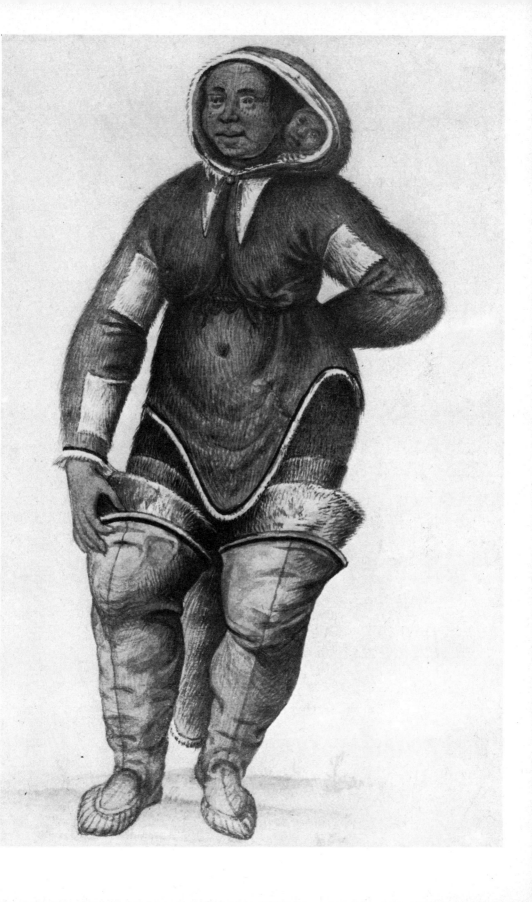

Despite this apparent setback, English expeditions to the Hudson Bay region continued, with at least enough success to result in 1670 in a royal charter to the 'Company of Merchant Adventurers, Trading into Hudson's Bay'.

And so by the beginning of the eighteenth century Eskimos had been encountered by Europeans in Greenland, on the east coast of America from Labrador northward, and to the west in Hudson Bay, and enterprises had been set in motion that would ensure their continued intercourse.

THE RUSSIANS

While the English were making their preliminary discoveries around Hudson Bay, the Russians had moved relentlessly eastwards over the great landmass of Siberia, lured not by the fabled riches of the Orient, but rather by the immediate prospect of obtaining furs. By 1700 they had reached the Pacific, and were poised to extend explorations to a whole new continent rumoured to lie beyond the sea. In his first Pacific voyage of discovery in 1728, Vitus Bering sailed under royal commission northwards from the Kamchatka Peninsula to Bering Strait and returned. He stopped briefly at St Lawrence Island, where he encountered Eskimos. In 1732 a brief landing on American soil was claimed by men of an expedition under Mikhail Gvozdev and Ivan Fedorof, but if it really occurred, it was inconsequential.

More important, in 1730 Bering proposed to the Russian empress further explorations that would lead specifically to the discovery of sea routes to America and Japan. The proposal was accepted, and in 1733 the staff of the Second Kamchatka Expedition left St Petersburg, headed by Bering, seconded by Alexei Chirikof, and including a substantial representation of scientists who would further the work of intelligent discovery. Supply of the enormous undertaking was difficult, the building of ships on the Pacific even more so. The expedition was not in fact seaworthy until 1740, and its two vessels did not finally set sail for America from their base at Petropavlovsk for still another year.

Then, misled in their directions by faulty if imaginative maps of the unknown area, the ships were shortly separated from one another. Chirikof made land on 15 July 1741, apparently in what is now south-eastern Alaska. A day or so later Bering, in the other ship, sighted Mount St Elias. Chirikof succeeded in returning to Petropavlovsk after the loss of some of his men in their first encounter with American natives – probably Indians – and after meeting others somewhere in the Aleutian chain of islands. He obtained a few furs.

Bering was less fortunate. After a brief stop at Kayak Island, where evidence of natives was found, and after meeting Aleuts in the Shumagin Islands, the ship was wrecked in a November storm on what is now Bering Island of the Commander group, west of the Aleutian Islands. Here Bering died. A portion of the crew survived the winter, living chiefly on sea mammals, and the following year built a boat from the wreckage of the ship, in which they succeeded in reaching Petropavlovsk. With them they took furs of the animals – including sea otter – that had provided their winter subsistence.

The response to the furs was immediate. In 1743, 1745, 1747, and 1749 crews under one Emilian Bassof sailed in a small boat from Kamchatka to the Commanders, each time wintering over, and each time returning with a small fortune. Others followed. In September 1745 Mikhail Nevodchikof sailed to Agattu in the Near Islands of the Aleutians, was repulsed by unfriendly natives, and moved to Attu to remain a year, meeting various Aleuts and killing at least fifteen. Voyages continued to the Commanders, and the Near Islands were visited again by 1748 or 1749. Beginning in the latter year one ship passed four years in the Aleutians. In 1753 at least one visit was made to the eastern Aleutians, while in 1759 a ship wintered on Umnak in the Fox Islands and in 1761 a crew wintered on the Alaska Peninsula, where they experienced difficulty with the natives.

By the 1760s sailings were commonplace. Trustworthy accounts indicate there were more than eighty sailings to the Commanders, the Aleutians, and the Pribilof Islands during the second half of the eighteenth century, and that vessels averaged three to four years on each trip. Thus between 1760 and 1790 – the most active period for private hunters – there was an average of some seven Russian vessels in the islands at all times.

The operations included hunting by Russian crews, hunting by impressed native crews, trade with the natives, and the collection of a tax from each native male on behalf of the Russian government. In 1762 the

3   Sketch of the harbour at Three Saints, Kodiak Island, 1790. Three Saints was the major Russian settlement on the island for the decade following its establishment in 1783, when it was replaced by the new capital, St Paul, at the present town of Kodiak, Alaska. Paddlers in the double-cockpitted skin boats are wearing the typical Kodiak hat with sloping brim, woven of roots. This drawing derives from the Russian voyage under Joseph Billings, which reached Three Saints on 29 June, 1790; tents set up by the crew appear at the far left.

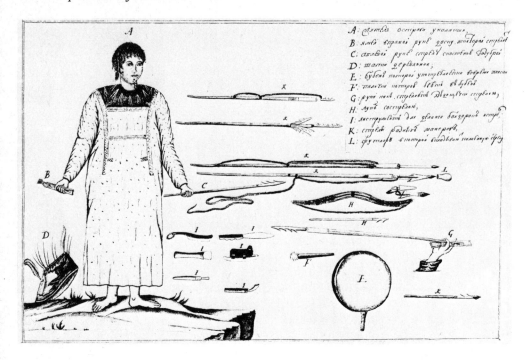

The key text alongside the drawing:

A: *слетя остреа уналатие*
B: *нлетя выраны рупъ госпя сепеторы стрелет*
C: *аелеея рупъ стрелеи спасеетно боербра*
D: *шатет зербленея*
E: *бубенъ которои употребленеи бобрыи плаеи*
F: *палетеи которой бетни бубенъ*
G: *рупъ паетъ стрелетеи ббомушти стрелети*
H: *лунъ састреами*
I: *инструшенты дла делаея бабдарой астре*
K: *стрелет родлеия манеровъ*
L: *футларъ втоторои ваоблении тольтотъ ефта*

4 An Aleut man from Unalaska, with some of his equipment. According to the key, B is a throwing stick or throwing board; C, a barbed dart; D, a wooden hat (a visor, often with open crown, worn in the skin boat, as in Ills. 9 and 11); E and F, drum and drumstick; G, demonstration of the use of the throwing board; H, bow and arrow; I, instruments for making kayaks and spears; K, various kinds of darts (of which the lowest is a toggling harpoon); L, sheath for dart blade. Drawing by Lieutenant Mikhail Levashef, 1767.

Aleuts of the Fox Islands rose and butchered a number of Russian hunters. Retaliation was swift and harsh.

The Aleutian Islands gained, expansion to the east was more difficult. When Stephan Glotov wintered on Kodiak Island in 1763, he found the natives – whom he noted to speak a language unintelligible to his Aleut hunters, but who had apparently heard all they wanted to of the Russians – so aggressive that it was not possible to leave the ship to hunt. The experiment was repeated by a ship in 1775 and another in 1779, with the same unprofitable result. In 1783 three ships set out for Prince William Sound to establish a permanent camp, but they too were immediately forced to leave by unfriendly natives – who, like their cousins of Kodiak, were speakers of Eskimo, but who in the typical foreigner's view that all natives are the same, would continue to be referred to by the Russians as 'Aleuts'.

Settlements in the new region did come, however. In the year of the repulse in Prince William Sound, Russians under Gregori Shelikof settled forcibly at Three Saints Bay on southern Kodiak Island, and thereafter Kodiak was never without a Russian post. By 1799, when a monopoly on trade and hunting in the new colonial area was granted by the Russian crown to the Russian America Company, there were more or less permanent stations on Kodiak, the Alaska Peninsula, the Kenai Peninsula and in Prince William Sound.

And so by the close of the eighteenth century the homeland of the Eskimo-Aleut peoples on the north Pacific had been explored – from Attu on the west, to Prince William Sound on the east.

UNITY OF PEOPLES

Inasmuch as the early European explorers of the north-east of America were wont to think of Greenland and Labrador as extensions of Asia, it is not surprising that they should have taken the Eskimos to be Asian people – nor would physical appearance belie such an opinion. According to one of Frobisher's captains, Christopher Hall, 'they be like to Tartars, with long blacke haire, broad faces, and flatte noses, and tawnie in colour, wearing Seale skinnes. . . . The women are marked in the face with blewe streakes downe the cheekes, and round about the eies.' It is even less surprising that the naturalist George Wilhelm Steller, a member of Bering's second expedition, assumed on the basis of their appearance that the Aleuts of the Shumagin Islands were related to the natives of Kamchatka, although he also noted the similarity of their skin-covered boats to those of the Greenland Eskimos.

In 1819 a Dutch scholar, Rasmus Rusk, wrote the first comparative study of the Aleutian and Greenland languages, in which he concluded that they were related. During that same century, explorations by Russians in Norton Sound and to the north in Alaska, by Americans on the Alaskan Arctic coast, and by British in the great central Canadian regions led to more and more reports about Eskimos. In the 1880s the first scientific ethnographic studies of Eskimos were made in East Greenland and Baffinland, and at the same time the Danish linguist Hinrich Rink wrote with conviction of the relationships of the Eskimos and Aleuts linguistically and culturally, and argued that Eskimo culture had originated in Alaska, and spread thence to Greenland. Yet it was not until nearly a decade after the close of the nineteenth century that the last major group of central Canadian Eskimos was discovered by Vilhjalmur Stefansson in the Coronation Gulf region. And it was still another decade before the process of discovery was complete, when in the early 1920s the Fifth Thule Expedition under Knud Rasmussen performed a traverse of the entire American north from Greenland to Alaska, studying, collecting, excavating, and finally underscoring the ultimate ethnic unity of the peoples living across the top of the American world.

THE LAND

It seems fitting that the boundary of the Eskimos on the east is marked by ice – the great Polar ice pack that flows southwards along the eastern shore of Greenland so thick that even in summer ships seldom sail. But to the inhabitants of Greenland the pack ice brought sea animals, polar bears and driftwood, rafted countless days over a measureless distance from far to the west.

The only part of Greenland that in the warmer seasons is free of ice and snow is a narrow coastal strip sloping mountainously to the sea from ranges that confine the enormous ice-cap; this strip is as much as 160 kilometres wide in the south-west, even wider in the extremely dry north-east. Predominant vegetation is low tundra, with some birch, willow, and alder in the relatively warmer and better-watered south-west. To the Norse, it was the southern areas which provided pasturage and sea products; to the Eskimos, the whole region, at one time or another, provided sea mammals, caribou, or musk oxen.

The Eskimo region of Canada, with the exception of some rugged mountains of bare rock that rise more than 2000 metres from Baffin and Ellesmere Islands, is mainly low and tundra-covered, with rounded hills. Remnants of glaciation – eskers and drumlins – radiate from earlier centres of ice, and straits between islands of the archipelago may still be ice-choked all the year round. Generally the mainland and Arctic islands are poorly drained and swampy in summer, with numerous lakes and streams, where char or Atlantic salmon provide an important food resource. The tree-line coincides closely with the southern boundary of Eskimo occupation, and for most Eskimos timber has been scarce.

The topography is more varied in Alaska. In the north, a tundra plain reminiscent of northern Canada slopes to the Arctic Ocean from the largely treeless Brooks Range, now free of permanent ice, in which a few peaks rise to elevations of 3000 metres. Across southern Alaska is the ridge of the Alaska Range which, although including Mt McKinley and a few other high peaks, is in most places no more than about 3000 metres in elevation. In the west, the rugged and glaciated Alaska Range merges with the Aleutian Range, comprising more than eighty volcanoes which extend along the Alaska Peninsula and into the sea as the Aleutian Islands, reaching for more than 1700 kilometres towards Asia. Nearly half the volcanoes are known to have been active within the last two hundred years.

Between the mountain ridges to north and south – the Brooks and Alaska ranges – lies a great plate of flat lowlands and relatively low but rough and wooded uplands through which flow two major rivers: the Yukon, rising in Canada, and the Kuskokwim, rising in the interior uplands of Alaska. Like other streams that debouch into the Bering Sea, these rivers receive massive runs of Pacific salmon that travel far inland, providing food that in both its richness and its regularity is unrivalled in the northward-flowing streams of northernmost Alaska or even of Canada.

Yet farther west, the Chukchi Sea forms a southward extension of the Arctic Ocean, and finds its southern boundary at Bering Strait, whence the Bering Sea stretches to the south-westward-trending Alaska Peninsula and the chain of Aleutian Islands, where it yields to the Pacific Ocean proper. With the exception of a relatively few coastal dwellers maintaining a toe-hold on the extreme eastern edge of the Chukchi Peninsula, this continuous water marks the western boundary of the Eskimo and Aleut peoples.

NATIVE ASIAN-AMERICANS

The Eskimo-Aleuts lived widely dispersed across this landscape, a string of not altogether homogeneous peoples extending from Attu Island at

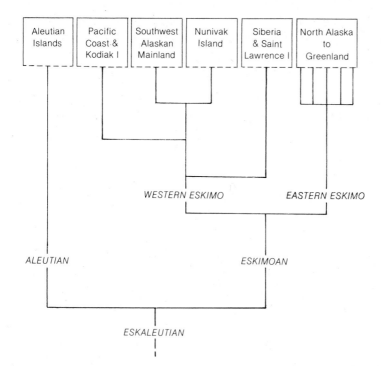

```
┌──────────┐┌──────────┐┌──────────┐┌──────────┐┌──────────┐┌──────────┐
│ Aleutian ││ Pacific  ││Southwest ││ Nunivak  ││ Siberia  ││North Alaska│
│ Islands  ││ Coast &  ││ Alaskan  ││ Island   ││ & Saint  ││    to     │
│          ││ Kodiak I ││ Mainland ││          ││Lawrence I││ Greenland │
└──────────┘└──────────┘└──────────┘└──────────┘└──────────┘└──────────┘
```

WESTERN ESKIMO   EASTERN ESKIMO

ALEUTIAN   ESKIMOAN

ESKALEUTIAN

5 A generalized family tree of Eskaleutian languages. No attempt is made to indicate all dialectal divisions, some of which apparently disappeared during the early years of contact with Europeans.

the extreme western end of the Aleutian chain to the eastern coast of Greenland – a distance of more than 7,000 kilometres as the crow flies, 11,000 kilometres by reasonably direct coastal-water routes, or sub-stantially more if one paddles Eskimo-fashion along the undulating shorelines.

Physically, there is considerable variation. Physical anthropologists find broad-headed individuals to be much more common in southern Alaska than elsewhere, and report some observable differences between most Eskimos on the one hand and most Aleuts on the other – differences such as in the height of the cranial vault. These variations seem to pale into insignificance, however, when matched against the similarities. Genetically, the Eskimo-Aleuts are the most Asian of all native Americans and have been classed together with peoples of northern Siberia as Arctic Mongoloids, a physical type said to be distinctive enough for skeletons to be consistently distinguished from those of American Indians, except where intermarriage with Indians has occurred.

Linguistically, there is also diversity. Although the speech of all Eskimos and Aleuts is classified within a single Eskaleutian stock, there is a cleavage between Eskimoan and Aleutian that has been compared in its depth to that between English and Russian within the Indo-European language group. Aleutian, reportedly having consisted at the arrival of the Russians of two or three mutually intelligible dialects, was spoken throughout the Aleutian Islands and as far east as a point on the Alaska Peninsula at about the 159th degree of west longitude. From here

5, 6

6 The distribution of Eskaleutian languages in historical times. The inset also shows pertinent topography of Alaska.

north-eastward along the Peninsula, on Kodiak Island and around Prince William Sound, and northward from the Peninsula around the Alaskan coast and thence across Canada to Greenland, lived speakers of Eskimoan, a language family consisting of two mutually unintelligible languages, one of which has dialectal divisions within it nearly marked enough to justify the recognition of a third tongue.

This latter language, Western Eskimo, has been classified into as many as four dialects – one of the Pacific coastal region, a second of the Bering Sea coast from Bristol Bay to St Michael on Norton Sound, a third of Nunivak Island, and the fourth and most divergent, the speech

MERCATOR PROJECTION

miles 1000   2000

kms.   2000

Arctic Ocean

ARCTIC ARCHIPELAGO

ELLESMERE I.

GREENLAND

BAFFIN

Coronation Gulf

BARREN GROUNDS

CANADA

HUDSON BAY

LABRADOR

(U. S. A.)

ARCTIC CIRCLE

80°

70°

60°

■ speakers of
ALEUT

▨ speakers of
WESTERN ESKIMO

░ speakers of
EASTERN ESKIMO

of people of St Lawrence Island and of the Asian Eskimos at the tip of
the Chukchi Peninsula. Between St Michael and Unalakleet lies the
boundary with Eastern Eskimo, a much more homogeneous language
that embraces all speech of all Eskimos from Unalakleet northward and
eastward some 10,000 kilometres to Greenland. Within Eastern Eskimo
the dialectal differences are slight enough, for instance, for the Fifth
Thule Expedition's Greenland-born Knud Rasmussen, who had
spoken Greenland Eskimo since childhood, to have been able to
converse fairly freely throughout the entire distance from Greenland to
Norton Sound.

In a situation strikingly similar to that indicated by their physical characteristics, the Eskaleutian linguistic stock has also been said to be related to the speech stock of north-eastern Siberia, which includes the language of the Chukchi peoples. The divergence between Chukchi speech on the one hand and the Eskaleutian stock on the other has been suggested to be of about the same magnitude as that between Eskimoan and Aleutian within Eskaleutian. The possibility that this is true – that Eskimoan, Aleutian, and Chukchi may be three coordinate divisions of the same language stock – may have important implications for the prehistory of Eskaleut peoples, as will be discussed in our final chapter.

As one might expect with factors such as the distance involved, the variations in habitat, and the time apparently required for the linguistic divergence of the various Eskaleut peoples, there was considerable variation in ways of life. Even within the area of Eastern Eskimo speech – the uniformity of which suggests that only a relatively short time has elapsed since its ancestral speakers formed a single social group – the diversity is notable.

Only in northern Canada, among the so-called Central Eskimos between Coronation Gulf and Baffinland, was there practised the way of life so often thought of as 'Eskimo' – people without permanent houses in any season, spending the winter in snow-block structures known to speakers of English as 'igloos'. In winter, these domed, snow-block houses were located on the offshore ice to allow seal-hunting at scattered breathing-holes, or in some cases were situated to permit hunting of the Barren Grounds caribou or, where available, the musk oxen. In summer, tents allowed flexibility in the chase for caribou, or in visits to seasonal fishing spots. Mobility was important in all cases.

7 Labrador Eskimo man paddling a kayak, an inflated sealskin behind him on the boat. Watercolour by Peter Rindisbacher, 1821.

Both eastward and westward from the Central Eskimos – in Greenland, in Labrador and parts of Baffinland, and in Alaska – winters were spent in semi-subterranean houses ('iglus') of sod or stone. Although winter sealing through the ice was practised, and might on occasion require temporary camps in snow-block shelters, it was less important in these regions, permitting the establishment of permanent winter settlements. Summers, on the other hand, would see a move to tents, and a mobile quest for land mammals such as caribou or musk oxen, or for sea mammals in coastal waters with the use of the single-seated skin kayak. At favourable locations in Greenland, Labrador and northern Alaska, great whales were hunted by crews from the large open skin boat, the *umiak*; the whale was repeatedly harpooned, forced to drag lines to which were attached inflated bladders of sealskin, until finally, exhausted, it was killed with a lance and towed ashore and butchered amidst joyous ritual. So similar were the techniques used in both east and west that it is clear they were inherited from an ancestral people who practised them throughout most of Arctic Canada, until climatic changes

8   Alaskan Eskimos in an umiak at King Island, in the Bering Strait region; an inflated sealskin drags astern; date unknown.

7

8

during the last few centuries altered the whale migrations and forced the Central Eskimos into their more mobile way of life based upon the taking of smaller game.

But not all Eastern Eskimo-speakers were coastal residents. In northern Alaska, some lived all or most of the year in the interior along major rivers or in the Brooks Range, where they hunted caribou and fished. They obtained necessary coastal products such as sea-mammal oil by trade or by the briefest of seasonal expeditions to the coast, wintering inland either in sod-covered houses or in a kind of double-walled, insulated tent. In the Barren Grounds of central Canada, indeed, one small group of Eskimos is reported to have stayed in the interior always, hunting caribou and fishing, wintering in snow-block houses, and making use of no sea products whatever. This is an exceptional case, however, for all other Eskimos required at least the oil of sea mammals to burn, to eat, and so to make life worth living.

On the islands around Bering Strait – St Lawrence and smaller ones – the hunting of land mammals tended to be much reduced, with people living by the pursuit of seal and walrus in skin boats in summer and some sealing and fishing through the ice in winter. But in most cases around the shores of Bering Sea, both on the coast and in upstream regions, a major focus was upon the taking of seasonally migrating fish. Here Pink and Chum salmon entered the shorter streams, the great King salmon swam prodigious distances up the major rivers, and huge runs of Sockeye salmon swarmed up streams to the lake systems around Bristol Bay. This great resource was supplemented – occasionally even equalled in importance – by caribou in the interior and by sea mammals on the coast.

In this entire zone discussed so far, then – from Greenland across Arctic Canada to Alaska, and along the Alaskan coast as far south as the Alaska Peninsula – there was practised a versatile economy using caribou, musk oxen when present, sea mammals large and small, and lake and river fish. The majority of these food sources were available to at least some extent in most places, and were acquired by means of similar techniques; but the particular emphasis might be varied radically to suit local conditions.

Despite the diversity of landforms, this great area has a number of characteristic features. It is predominantly tundra, rather than northern forest. More important, possibly, it comprises land in reasonable proximity to a sea coast that either freezes in winter or accumulates substantial amounts of drift ice. Indeed, with the exception of the south coast of Hudson Bay, which was inhabited by Algonquian-speaking Indians, speakers of Eskimo languages occupied the entire coast of North America that is consistently ice-bound in winter. In this respect the distribution of the Eskimo closely resembles that of the walrus.

Only at the Alaska Peninsula do these gross ecological characteristics change. The Eskimo-speakers of Prince William Sound, the tip of the Kenai Peninsula, Kodiak Island and the Pacific coast of the Alaska Peninsula, together with their western cousins the Aleuts, inhabit an

area dominated by the Pacific maritime climate, in which even the most fjorded bays seldom or never freeze, in which summers are cool, overcast, and rainy, and in which the walrus is replaced by the great Steller sea lion, whose distribution does not accord with that of the Eskimo-Aleuts, but which extends far to the south along the Pacific coast of America. Here all sea-mammal hunting is on the open sea, made rich not only by migrations of bearded and fur seals, but also by non-migratory seals, sea lions, and sea otter which live upon nutrients supplied by upwelling currents along the Aleutian Trough. Short, rapid streams, even far out in the Aleutians, receive substantial runs of Chum salmon, and coastal streams on Kodiak also experience massive migrations of Sockeye. Like their northern relatives, most of these peoples (except on northern Kodiak and the Kenai Peninsula) lived away from trees, as a result not of Arctic cold, but of the cool, insular Aleutian conditions. Land mammals on Kodiak Island included the great Alaska Brown Bear, which on the mainland was joined by the caribou, but these large mammals did not occur westwards beyond Unimak Island in the extreme eastern Aleutians.

9 Aleuts returning from a sea-otter hunt at Unalaska Island, probably in the 1890s.

9

10 Interior of a habitation
on Unalaska Island, 1778,
with a portion of the roof cut
away to show construction. A
number of the inhabitants are
seated in the shallow trough-
like sleeping and sitting zone
around the periphery of the
dwelling (see Ill. 44).
Drawing by John Webber,
1778.

11   Aleutian tradition: ornamented hunter's hat of wood. Similar hats were worn by kayak paddlers throughout western Alaska, and related visors are worn by the Aleut paddlers in Ill. 9.

It is not too surprising that in this zone hunting techniques differed somewhat from those of the northern Eskimos. Much hunting was by means of the two-holed kayak, in which the forward man could manage darts while the man aft managed the boat. Here the umiak was used only for freight and travel and whale-hunting was by dart alone, thrown from the kayak, rather than by harpoon. Dead whales were not captured but were allowed to die and drift up somewhere along the stretch of mainland and islands. While there is no absolutely clear evidence, aconite whale poison is believed to have been used on these darts. Houses were, as usual, most often semi-subterranean, but here they often lacked entrance passages: on Kodiak, multi-roomed houses might be entered through the side, almost directly; in the Aleutian region houses were entered by ladder through the roof.

In these ways, then, the Pacific Eskimos and the Aleuts formed a kind of unit, despite linguistic differences between the two, and to an extent were set apart from their northern brethren and cousins. On the other hand, the hunting complex was by no means totally distinct from that found in the north. Indeed, in their strong emphasis on boatmanship and open-water-hunting, these peoples resembled the later Eskimos of southern Greenland.

On more social and intellectual levels there were also broad similarities: there were no 'chiefs' as such, but influential individuals who were respected because of innate ability and of their virtuosity in such acquired skills as were available to everyone. Control of the anti-social was maintained through the influence of such individuals, through supportive ties with kinfolk, and through similar but more fictional ties inherent in a great variety of 'partnerships' contracted between non-kin. These same ties contributed to survival in hard times and to a general prosperity in good, because of the working through them of traditional devices for sharing food and other resources. Although broadly pragmatic, practical and addicted to the invention and use of material gadgets in profusion, each person carried on a certain discourse with supernatural forces by means of song, amulets, and verbal formulae. The most adept were set apart as practising shamans, capable of healing, of foretelling the future and sometimes of enlivening the long winter evenings with shows of magic, mummery and sleight of hand.

The implications thus of language, of physique and of culture are that Eskimos and Aleuts once formed a single people, who in the fullness of their prehistory had spread apart and taken somewhat different paths. This book is the outline of their story.

CHAPTER II

People of the Early Tundra

Given the linguistic relationship between Eskimos and Aleuts, it is reasonable to hope that archaeology will provide evidence of the time in which they were one people – something approximating a single great social group, practising a single way of life and characterized by a single coherent assemblage of tools. It is with this hope in mind that we shall look at the earliest cultural remains in the region.

The Eskimo region in particular, including the lengthy Arctic zone from Point Barrow to eastern Greenland, was not fully colonized by human beings until about 2000 bc, by which time – it now seems clear – both ancestral Eskimos and ancestral Aleuts were to be found in substantially the same areas that they inhabited upon the arrival of the Europeans. And, as will be shown in later chapters, the archaeological remains of the ancestral Aleuts and northern Eskimos are radically different from each other as early as 2000 bc, indicating umistakably that social differentiation had occurred a considerable time before.

Archaeological complexes earlier than 2000 bc are relatively few in number, and because of the glacial history of northern North America there was a long period of time in which human occupation was impossible over much of the area.

LATE PLEISTOCENE GLACIAL HISTORY

The Late Wisconsin glacial epoch dates from about 23,000 to 11,000 years ago, or 21,000 to 9000 bc in the uncorrected radiocarbon chronology. Maximum ice advance occurred about 18,000 to 16,000 bc.

12   The ice accumulated particularly heavily in areas surrounding Hudson Bay, where the eastern or Laurentide ice sheet was fed by moisture from the Gulf of Mexico and the North Atlantic. A smaller, thinner ice sheet lay over the northern portion of the Arctic Archipelago, making contact with the Greenland ice sheet on one side and the Laurentide ice on the other.

In western North America, Cordilleran ice extended outwards from the main mountain chains, reaching south to just below the present U.S./Canadian border, thrusting west well into the waters of the Gulf of Alaska, joining the Alaska Range and the eastern Aleutian range into a solid, south Alaskan ice-cap in the north, and coalescing with the Laurentide ice sheet in the east. The extent and duration of this mid-

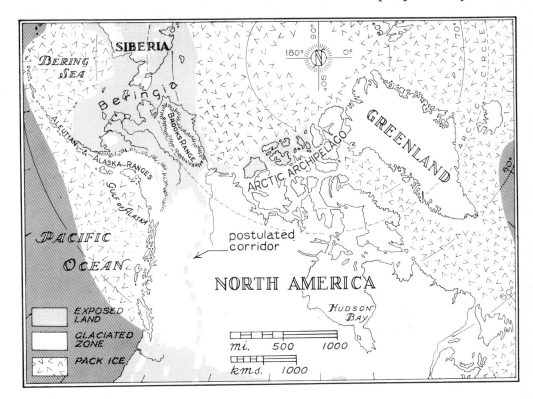

12 Land and sea ice of the late Pleistocene in relation to Beringia and modern landmasses.

continental coalescence, however, is the subject of debate. According to one view, it was only during the most pronounced glacial episodes of the Pleistocene that the Cordilleran and Laurentide ice actually abutted one another, so that during most of the Wisconsin epoch there was an open, ice-fringed passage leading from Alaska to the heart of North America. According to a second view, however, the corridor was closed most of the time, as the major North American ice sheets were jammed together, leaving a pathway to the south only for various fluctuating periods before about 23,000 bc and after a date that may be as late as 6500 bc. Each of these views carries its own implications for the prehistory both of Alaska and of North America.

In any event, north and west of the Cordilleran ice mass lay a largely glacier-free inland Alaska, a bowl set off by the continuous ice of the mountain ridges to the south and north and by the Canadian ice-cap to the east. Farther west, eastern Siberia possessed some mountain and valley glaciers at high altitudes, but the only major cap was that of the Taimyr Peninsula, well to the west of the Lena River. The lowlands, including the Arctic coastal plain, were ice free.

At the height of glaciation, the mass of ice in North America alone exceeded that existing in present-day Antarctica. Moisture trapped in the great ice-caps of the Pleistocene, of which the North American one was only a single representative, resulted in a marked lowering of the levels of the world's oceans. Today, portions of the sea in the Bering

Strait area are less than 40 metres deep. A drop in sea level of only this amount would convert the floor of the Strait into dry land, and separate the Arctic and Pacific Oceans. At the period of greatest glaciation, in fact, the lowering in sea level was some 100 metres, resulting in the exposure not simply of a narrow bridge of land, but of an expanse of continental shelf some 1500 kilometres wide at its narrowest north-to-south dimension. It is now thought that all or part of this shelf was exposed between about 23,000 and 12,000 bc, with some additional alternating periods of lesser exposure and minor inundation occurring between 12,000 and 8000 bc, after which the seas have been joined continuously.

The Pleistocene environment of this broad shelf, known as Beringia, was a continuation of that of the lowlands of eastern Siberia – dry tundra-steppe, with grassy tracts scattered among areas of more herbaceous tundra and marsh vegetation. Game included numerous grazing animals, such as woolly mammoth, horse and bison, in greater numbers than browsing animals such as moose, caribou and elk, suggesting that the tundra was grassier than that now common in the Arctic. Central and northern Beringia are thought to have had a dry climate, with short, relatively warm summers, severe winters and constant wind. The southern coast, at that time the northern edge of the Bering Sea, would have been cooled in summer by a cold and foggy sea, in winter by a certain amount of pack ice. Alaska and Beringia, then, were in a continental sense Asian rather than American, part of a great treeless, tundra-covered peninsula stretching from Asia eastwards to the vast ice sheets of North America.

By about 11,000 years ago, or 9000 bc, the North American glaciers were in swift retreat. By 5500 bc the main ice sheet over Canada had shrunk to two residual ice-caps, one on each side of Hudson Bay, to disappear finally about 2500 bc. In Alaska, mountain glaciers in the Brooks Range may have been of substantial size as late as 5000 bc. In the south, along the Alaska and Aleutian Ranges, where some glaciers remain today, the recession did not apparently reach its present stage until as late as 4000 bc in some areas, although others seem to have been substantially free of ice as early as 8000 bc.

THE EARLIEST ARCHAEOLOGICAL REMAINS

13 Modified caribou tibia tentatively identified as a flesher – a device for removing flesh from hides – from Old Crow Flats, in north-western Canada; the apatite fraction of the lower portion of the artifact, as it is shown here, has been radiocarbon dated to about 25,000 bc; length, about 25.5 cm.

In view of this glacial history, it is not surprising that northern Canada has produced no cultural remains that pre-date 5000 bc, and that before this date the sites from Alaska appear to reflect the position of the territory as an Asian appendage.

Within Alaska, there is clear evidence after 4000 bc of a differentiation between the tools of prehistoric inhabitants of the interior and those of the coast, and by then the Eskaleut ancestors can be expected to have been among coastal, rather than inland, peoples. Before that date, however, any such expectation is presumptive at best, and the earlier cultural backgrounds of these people who came to occupy the coast is not altogether clear. In the sections that follow the evidence for all cultural manifestations before 4000 bc will be surveyed briefly. The earliest securely dated occupation sites – although not the earliest artifacts – are of about 8000 bc, or perhaps a millennium earlier, and some other putatively early sites are still not satisfactorily placed in time. First, however, will be described what are apparently the earliest artifacts now known from the region.

Located about 50 kilometres east of the modern border between Alaska and the Yukon Territory of Canada is the locality called Old Crow Flats; this was part of the unglaciated heart of Alaska at the time it formed an extension of Asia during the Wisconsin epoch. Eroding sediments of the Old Crow River produced a collection of fossil animal bone; half of the eighteen species represented are now extinct in the region, and their extinct forms are divisible into two groups – one that includes species derived from Asia and probably adapted to the cold (such as woolly mammoth), and the other, species derived from southern North America and probably adapted to a warmer climate (such as mastodon and camelid). The two groups are considered to be about the same age, suggesting that they lived during a transitional period from a warm to a cooler climate.

Among the animal bones, and like them presumed to have been redeposited by stream action, are a number of modified bones thought to be artifacts. One of them, in particular, interpreted as a flesher or implement for cleaning hides, has a spatulate end with unmistakable carving, presumably done with a stone tool. A search of the region for a stone assemblage that might relate to the bone artifacts has thus far yielded nothing of apparently equivalent age.

13

The bone of three of the artifacts has yielded radiocarbon dates between about 24,000 and 27,000 bc, with variance estimates of up to 3,000 years. Other unmodified bone in the collection gave comparable dates. Despite the unreliability of many radiocarbon determinations from bone, the investigators of the site attest their confidence in the sophisticated treatment of their material in the radiocarbon laboratory, and conclude that the presence of man is indicated, before the peak of the late Wisconsin glaciation. Their conclusion finds some support in excavations of recent years in Mexico and the Peruvian Andes, which have produced radiocarbon evidence – although unfortunately not altogether unambiguous – of the presence of man in these parts of America before 20,000 years ago.

No similarly early dates have been obtained elsewhere in the Alaskan region. The nearest approach is a radiocarbon determination from bison bones at the Trail Creek caves of the Seward Peninsula, thought to have been broken by humans in order to remove the marrow; the date is about 13,000 bc. All other late Pleistocene tool complexes in the general area are younger and, with the exception of one virtually complete and six fragmentary bone points from the Trail Creek caves, no bone tools have survived in them.

THE PALAEO-ARCTIC TRADITION

The artifact assemblages that are here assigned to the Palaeo-arctic tradition are somewhat varied, but consistently characteristic artifacts

14 include microblades, small wedge-shaped cores from which the blades were pressed, some relatively generalized leaf-shaped or ellipsoidal bifaces and some of the grooving or scraping implements, commonly known as burins, made by careful longitudinal blows. The miniature cores, which have sometimes been called Campus-type microcores, from the site on the University of Alaska campus where they were first reported, have a narrow elliptical striking platform usually created by the removal of a transverse flake, from which bladelets have been pressed at one end; the edges opposite the striking platform and the fluted blade scars are worked into a sharp keel by either bifacial or unifacial flaking, presumably to facilitate wedging the core while pressing blades. The length of the blades removed usually does not exceed 5 centimetres. In these assemblages, there is little evidence for the use of stone projectile heads. It is assumed that most projectiles were of organic material, armed with microblade sections set in slots on the sides; in some collections microblade mid-sections, with one thick, flattened edge formed by chipping, predominate over all other blade fragments.

In addition to these consistently recurring artifacts, some of the assemblages also include larger blades struck from polyhedral cores, as

16 well as large and more-or-less discoidal bifaces used both as tools and as flake cores. Some of the bifaces were flaked peripherally to create a pronouncedly bulging side, which was then knocked off as a single pre-formed flake and used as a tool without further modification – a technique that can reasonably be termed Levallois. Besides these assemblages, there are others which may eventually be recognized as an integral part of this tradition, with well-formed and unmistakable stone projectile points; some, however, lack bifacially chipped stone entirely. For present purposes these assemblages will be discussed separately as variants of the Palaeo-arctic tradition.

15 Most of the sites clearly assignable to the Palaeo-arctic tradition are confined to areas untouched by the latest major local glacial episodes – some of which, as indicated earlier, may have persisted until 5000 bc. Best known of these assemblages are those termed the Akmak and Kobuk complexes from north-western Alaska. The first of these comprises, in addition to the wedge-shaped microcores, microblades, burins, and ellipsoidal bifaces, an additional group of artifacts that are relatively simple products of percussion chipping. They include a number of the large core bifaces referred to earlier, which apparently served not only as cores, but – at least in some cases – as heavy cutting or chopping implements; of larger polyhedral cores and blades struck or pressed from them; of large flakes retouched either bifacially or unifacially and apparently used as cutting implements; and of some grooved stones.

14   Palaeo-arctic tradition: blades and cores: *a*, *b*, cores of the Akmak complex, Onion Portage; *c*, core, *d*, *e*, blades, Ugashik Narrows phase, Ugashik River drainage on the Alaska Peninsula.

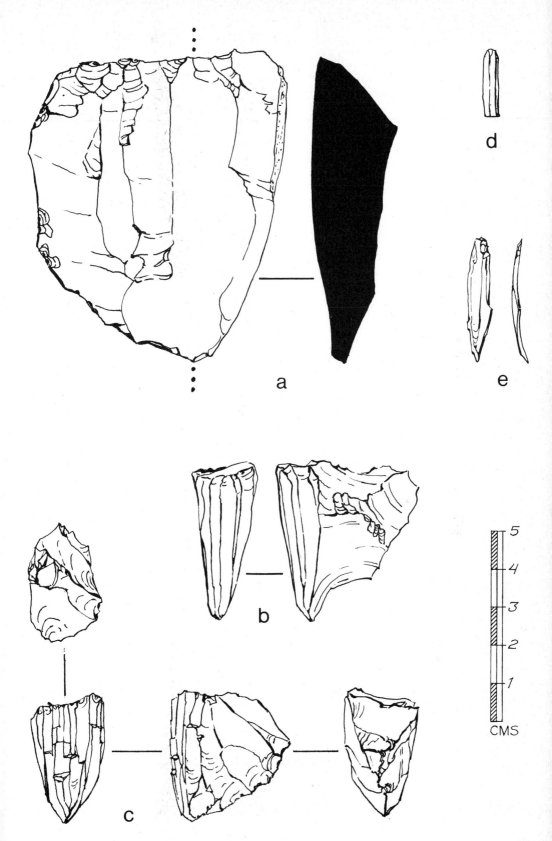

a

d

e

b

c

5
4
3
2
1
CMS

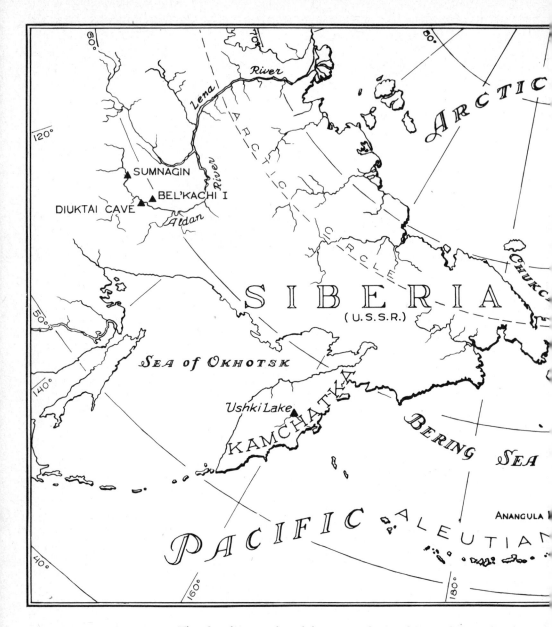

15　Locations mentioned in relation to the Palaeo-arctic tradition. In America outside Alaska, a few related complexes are known from eastern Yukon Territory and from British Columbia. Cultural affinities lie with Asia.

The first-discovered and best-attested assemblage of the Akmak complex is the earliest component of the deeply stratified site at Onion Portage on the Kobuk River, about 200 kilometres from the river's outlet on the Chukchi Sea. The artifacts are thought to have been left in the vicinity of some sort of dwelling which, unfortunately, was eroded away in antiquity. Bone believed to have been associated with the Akmak materials gave a radiocarbon date of about 8000 bc. Another site, located a few kilometres south of Barrow, has yielded bifaces apparently similar to the large core bifaces of the Onion Portage assemblage, as well as the smaller wedge-shaped microcores.

At Onion Portage, in part overlying the Akmak materials in convincing stratigraphic context, is a somewhat younger assemblage

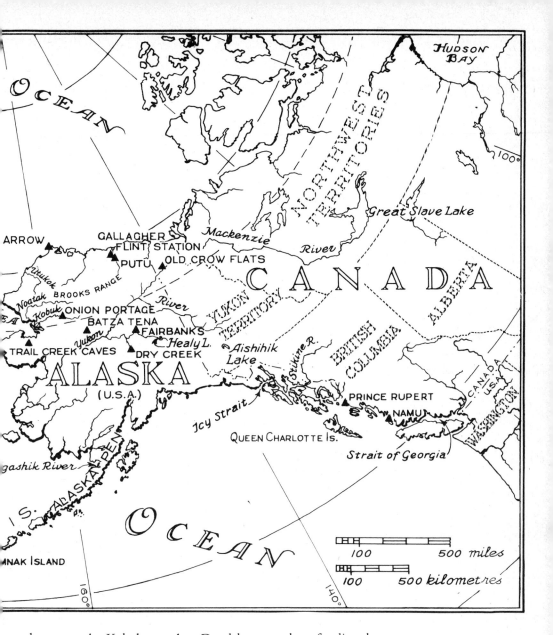

known as the Kobuk complex. Dated by a number of radiocarbon
determinations to about 6000 bc, the collection consists almost entirely of
the characteristic wedge-shaped microcores and the bladelets produced
from them, and is thought to represent less than the full inventory of
artifacts used by the people concerned. That is, the artifacts seem to mark
the remains not of a relatively permanent dwelling area, but of numerous
short-term, river-edge, caribou-hunting camp-sites.

From this vicinity other collections containing such microcores have
been made along the north slope of the Brooks Range near the
Kukpowruk and Utukok Rivers, as well as in the Noatak River
drainage. The lowest artifact-bearing levels of Trail Creek caves on the
Seward Peninsula have yielded blades similar to some of those derived

16 Palaeo-arctic tradition: small core biface from the Narrows phase, upper Ugashik River drainage, south-western Alaska; maximum breadth, 7 cm.

from the wedge-shaped microcores, as well as small, slender projectile heads of antler – arrowheads to judge by their size – which are grooved on the sides apparently to receive the microblade sections. The levels are dated by radiocarbon to about 7000 bc.

Eight hundred kilometres almost directly south of and across the breadth of Alaska from the area just mentioned, another assemblage assignable to the Palaeo-arctic tradition is known in the Ugashik River drainage on the Bering Sea side of the Alaska Peninsula. Here, at a narrow crossing between the two Ugashik lakes, has been recovered an assemblage dated to about 7000 bc, consisting of the same wedge-shaped microcores, microblades, burins, leaf-shaped bifaces and core bifaces as were found at other Palaeo-arctic locations.

In central Alaska, the Dry Creek site south-west of Fairbanks has yielded all the especially characteristic artifacts mentioned above – microblades, wedge-shaped cores, burins, leaf-shaped bifaces – and a single larger blade apparently removed from a prepared core. Located on outwash of what seems to be an early Wisconsin-age glaciation, the artifact-bearing zone has a radiocarbon age of about 8700 bc. Elsewhere in central Alaska, certain sites of the so-called 'Denali complex' have been shown to date from 8000 bc and earlier; these produced wedge-shaped microcores, blades derived from them, certain small flat burins, scrapers, and some bifacially flaked knives. The particular assemblages concerned are so similar in constituent artifacts and in radiocarbon dates to others assigned here to the Palaeo-arctic tradition that they also must be considered a part of it, although this is not the case with all assemblages to which the designation Denali complex has been applied.

The initial find of a Denali assemblage was from the campus of the University of Alaska, where the deposit yielded at least one side-notched projectile point, although such implements are thought by some investigators to be intrusive there. Similar assemblages in central Alaska and as far east as western Yukon Territory, most of which have also yielded side-notched or stemmed stone projectile points, have dates varying from 2500 bc to as late as 500 bc and even AD 1000; these also have been referred by at least some archaeologists to the Denali complex.

When compared with the much earlier dates mentioned for sites to the north-west and south-west, and with some others in central Alaska, these particular representatives of the Denali complex pose a problem. Considering the number of apparently valid but late radiocarbon dates, it is hardly likely that all such determinations represent mistakes either by laboratories or by excavators. It must be supposed, therefore, that some elements similar to those of the Palaeo-arctic tradition persisted in east-central Alaska as late as the beginning of the Christian era.

Considering specifically the evidence from the Akmak and Kobuk complexes, it seems possible that those assemblages in which a substantial proportion of the collection is formed by larger blades, cores, and discoidal core-bifaces will turn out to be consistently somewhat earlier than those in which they are lacking. Conclusive evidence of this is not yet to hand, however.

Palaeo-arctic Variants:
Sites with Specialized Projectile Points

At Healy Lake, south-west of Fairbanks in the Yukon-Tanana Uplands, excavations in an abandoned Athapaskan village revealed a shallow but apparently stratified site. Of the 40-centimetre-deep cultural material, the lowest 5 centimetres yielded an apparently distinctive complex known as *Chindadn,* from the Tanana Athapaskan word for ancestor. The collection, composed of about 150 implements, includes very thin, tear-drop-shaped or triangular points, 2.8–4.9 centimetres in length, with fairly straight sides and partly rounded bases; microblades; and a pair of burins. Bones of small animals and birds in the layer yielded a date of about 9000 bc. Chindadn points are unknown elsewhere, although the chipping technique has been compared to that on one lanceolate biface from the Akmak deposit at Onion Portage. A zone about 5 centimetres above the Chindadn level yielded additional bone from which was obtained a radiocarbon date of about 7000 bc. This zone, with a relatively light artifact yield, produced a pair of core-bifaces reminiscent of those, again, of the Akmak complex at Onion Portage.

Still other collections may contain stone projectile points with fluted bases. Because fluted points were used by so-called Palaeo-Indian hunters of now-extinct elephants and ancient bison farther south in North America – represented by the Clovis and Folsom assemblages – the Alaskan fluted lanceolate points have been claimed by some archaeologists to provide evidence of the migration of the ancestors of these Palaeo-Indians to the New World. As new evidence accumulates, however, this theory appears more and more questionable.

Surface finds of often rather crudely fluted points have been made in various Alaskan locations in the vicinity of the Brooks Range. In one surface site on the Utukok River, fragments of two such fluted implements were found together with four other lanceolate points, blades, blade cores, a discoidal core, and a single microblade. Pieces of elephant tusk in or on the site were dated to about 15,400 bc, whereas other mammal bone – probably of caribou – had a radiocarbon age of about 400 bc. In view of the superficial nature of the site, either date – or neither – may reflect the true age of the artifacts.

Fragments of other fluted points were discovered in a buried context at the Putu site in the Sagavanirktok River Valley. These were described as part of a complex including burins and large blades, and were compared by the excavator with the earliest materials of the Clovis-related Levi site in Texas. A radiocarbon determination on organic material in soil surrounding the artifacts provided a single date of about 6500 bc, which was rejected by the investigator as too young. Subsequent work at the site produced evidence of a microblade industry, however, and in view of the total artifact assemblage and its general similarity to others of the Palaeo-arctic tradition, the date from the soil may well provide an accurate estimate of the age of the site.

Similar fluted points were recovered at flaking stations in an obsidian-rich locality called Batza Tena, in the valley of the Koyukuk River,

17

17 Palaeo-arctic tradition: Chindadn points from Healy Lake; length of the longer, about 4.3 cm.

18

18 Palaeo-arctic tradition: fluted point found along the Utukok River in 1947; length, 5.5 cm.

where there is no convincing local dating evidence. Microblades were also unearthed in this locality, but it is not certain whether they were related to the fluted points, although it is reported that fluted points and microblades were found together at another, hitherto unpublished, site farther up the Koyukuk River valley. Altogether, the dating of fluted points in Alaska is not clear. Although it is possible that evidence will be forthcoming to show their contemporaneity with – or even greater age than – broadly similar implements in the continental United States (where they start as early as about 9500 bc), the present evidence hints at least as strongly that the relatively rare fluted points belong in assemblages of the Palaeo-arctic tradition, as it is both described and dated here.

Palaeo-arctic Variants: Sites without Bifaces

There are two important sites, widely separated in space and apparently also in time, in which the nature of the collections has suggested to some investigators a cultural affinity slightly outside that indicated by most assemblages of the Palaeo-arctic tradition.

The extensive Anangula site, located on an islet off the coast of Umnak Island in the Fox group of the eastern Aleutians, has been the focus of numerous seasons of work, and has yielded extensive remains of 19 a blade and core industry, scrapers, scraping implements made by a transverse burin blow, and fragments of stone vessels and of flat slabs upon which red ochre was pulverized. Although some wedge-shaped cores are present, most cores are variable in form, made without any serious attempt at shaping other than the flattening of a striking platform, often rotated in use so that multiple sets of blade facets are oriented in different directions. The cores are often of materials that have been called shaly chert or cherty shale. Unlike at least most of the other assemblages treated so far, there is no clear distinction between blades and microblades; although both large and small blades are included, sizes intergrade freely. Also unlike the other assemblages, there are no bifaces. Evidence is reported for the existence of houses, elliptical in plan, about 5 metres in length, partly excavated into the contemporary ground surface,

19   Palaeo-arctic tradition, Anangula variant: core and blades from Anangula Island, near Umnak Island in the Aleutians.

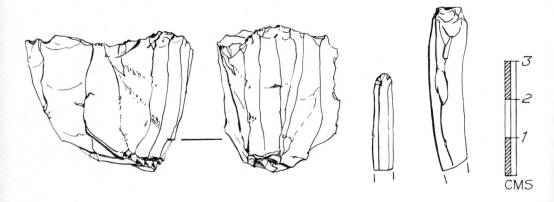

CMS

and presumably entered through the roof. An impressive series of radiocarbon determinations provides a date of about 6000 bc.

It was originally suggested that with the lowering of sea level at the height of the Wisconsin glacial period the Anangula site lay not on an island but at the edge of the landmass of Beringia itself, and that the inhabitants represented the ancient population which had occupied the southern fringe of this shelf. Such a location, as well as some fragments of sea-mammal bone in the site, was seen as evidence of an economic specialization in products of the sea coast at that early date. More recent information indicates that the sea had risen to approximately its present level before the site was occupied, a circumstance which would have required the use of boats by immigrants to Anangula. Thus the case for a coastal economic adaptation is fairly strong, even in the absence of an artifact complex which is specific to such a way of life. Furthermore, the apparent existence of permanently constructed houses at Anangula bespeaks a degree of sedentism that is not known from other sites of the Palaeo-arctic tradition. Palaeo-arctic sites, where settlement type can be determined at all and with the possible exception of the suspected dwelling at Onion Portage, mentioned above, usually seem to consist of temporary camps, often at obvious game crossings.

The second site without bifaces, known as the Gallagher Flint Station, lies in the region of the Sagavanirktok River north of the Brooks Range, and produced evidence of what has been described as a generalized core and blade industry, largely in calcareous siltstone or mudstone. As with the collection from Anangula, blade sizes and core styles vary widely, with cores often rotated so that sets of blade scars may be oriented in various directions on the same core; like Anangula, the assemblage contains no bifacial implements, but tools instead are confined to edge-trimmed flakes and blades. The use of burin blows to sharpen implements is not indicated, however. A single radiocarbon determination from charcoal in apparent association with the cultural material provides a date of about 8600 bc.

20 Palaeo-arctic tradition: blade core (two views) from the Gallagher Flint Station; height, 6 cm.

Thus, despite the time and space which separated them and the variation in the ecological zones in which they appeared, the Gallagher and Anangula collections exhibit numerous similarities in techniques of blade manufacture, in the materials chosen, and in the complete reliance upon unifacially made implements, although some Anangula tool-types are lacking at the Gallagher site. Given the differences between other assemblages of the Palaeo-arctic tradition, however, it is quite possible to regard them not as representing together some single culture, but rather as independent examples of one limit of the normal range of variation within the Palaeo-arctic tradition.

Cultural Relationships
Despite the relative paucity of archaeological work in the great area of north-eastern Asia, research in the past few years has been sufficient to provide indications of a prehistory of considerable complexity, and with clear relevance for that of the American Arctic.

On the basis of collections primarily from Diuktai Cave and the site of Bel'kachi I in the valley of the Aldan River – an eastern tributary of the Lena – one Soviet researcher has tentatively defined a Palaeolithic Diuktai culture, represented by bifacially chipped projectile heads (usually oval), and knives, disc-shaped cores, wedge-shaped blade cores, some Levallois cores, blades, microblades, scrapers and a variety of burins. Radiocarbon dates suggest a span from as early as about 20,000 to about 8000 bc.

According to the same investigator, levels V and VI of the site at Ushki Lake on the Kamchatka Peninsula, dating from and before about 8000 bc, represent a last, eastern stage of the Diuktai culture, which he assumes was spread throughout the extensive intervening region between Kamchatka and the middle Lena area. These levels of the Ushki site are reported to have produced bifacial knives, leaf-shaped projectile points, wedge-shaped cores and microblades, so that it seems clear that these elements were widespread in north-eastern Asia at the very end of the Pleistocene, apparently indicating an adaptation to the eastern Siberian tundra zone.

At about this same time, 8000 bc, the Diuktai culture in the middle Lena region was replaced by, or gave rise to, the Sumnagin culture, dating from 8000 to 4000 bc, which is taken to represent seasonal hunters and fishers who pursued both moose in the northern coniferous forest and reindeer on the tundra. Tools include crude choppers, scrapers, adzes, axes and numerous small blades detached from prismatic cores, but include no bifacially worked implements. Although some wedge-shaped cores occur, they are few in number. Farther east, the latest levels of the Ushki site produced an assemblage characterized by a variety of blade cores other than those of wedge shape, numerous large blades struck from them, some bifacial knives, various scrapers, flaked adzes and bifacially flaked stone projectile points, some of them stemmed.

The impression thus created, albeit on the basis of rather scanty information, is that during several millennia bracketing 8000 bc the artifact variety represented in northern Asia from the Lena basin eastwards is of the same kind as the variety within the early tool complexes of Alaska; and that there was an underlying theme of blade manufacture, chiefly but not always using wedge-shaped cores, with the frequent but not universal presence of bifaces of generalized shape, or of leaf-shaped, sometimes lanceolate, projectile blades.

Turning to north-central Canada, there are no very early sites. Around Great Slave Lake, for instance, no remains are known until about 5000 bc, and no stone industries include blade production of any significance before about 1000 bc, at which time there was an intrusion of peoples believed to have been ancestral Eskimos, who will be discussed at length later. Thus there is no indication of the presence of people of Palaeo-arctic tradition as far east as north-central Canada.

To the west, however, Canadian collections do include blades; some of these collections have been mentioned in connection with the Denali complex. In a site at Aishihik Lake in Yukon Territory, not far from the

Alaskan border, a blade industry has been dated to about 2500 bc. In south-west Yukon microblades are considered to be an integral part of collections that also include varieties of side-notched projectile points. Although the dating of these assemblages is not altogether certain, there seems to be valid radiocarbon evidence for the presence here of microblades produced from wedge-shaped cores at least as early as 1500 bc, and probably as early as 3000 bc. Another occurrence of microblades with stemmed and notched projectile points is reported a little farther eastwards, in the south-western portion of the Northwest Territories, where the dating can be assumed to be similar to that in Yukon Territory.

Farther south, and on the Pacific coast itself, wedge-shaped cores bearing a number of features resembling those of the Palaeo-arctic tradition are known from the Icy Strait region in south-eastern Alaska, where they date from about 6000 to 2000 bc, appearing in collections that include some unidentifiable bifacial implements unfortunately known so far only from fragments. Some 240 kilometres eastwards, beyond the Coast Mountains and near the upper Stikine River in what is now British Columbia, occurs the similar Ice Mountain Microblade phase, which is not yet adequately dated.

Still farther south, and still east of the coastal mountains, are found assemblages in which microblades, here no longer manufactured from the precise wedge-shaped cores of the Palaeo-arctic tradition, are associated with a variety of projectile points: these occur in the interior of British Columbia as early as 5000 bc, in south-central Washington by 4500 bc, but in Alberta remain undated.

On the coast itself again, the earliest known occupation of the Queen Charlotte Islands, about 5000 bc, is by people who made no bifacial stone tools at all, but who manufactured numerous microblades from cores chipped from pebbles or random flakes – a technique only barely reminiscent of the more precise procedures of the Palaeo-arctic tradition. Still farther south, at the site of Namu on the British Columbia coast, microblades and crude cores, together with some fragmentary bifacial stone implements, appear to date from as early as 7000 bc, when they seem to represent an occupation of terrestrial hunters. Some use of microblades apparently persisted at that site until 2000 bc.

Although blade-makers are not represented at all the earliest sites of the British Columbia coast – for instance, none are so far known in the vicinity of Prince Rupert – a healthy microblade tradition persisted in the Strait of Georgia region until about A D 400.

Summary:
A Siberian-American Palaeo-arctic Tradition
Long before 8000 bc, a variety of assemblages appeared in Asia with wedge-shaped cores, microblades and generalized projectile blades. By 8000 bc similar assemblages – collections of the Palaeo-arctic tradition – are known from Alaska, and are well within the range of variation of

assemblages of their Asian predecessors. These American collections occur either in or very near the zone that was left unglaciated during the late Pleistocene. Examples of later, presumably derivative, microblade industries occur in east-central Alaska, in extreme western Canada, and to the south, where they disappear at about the latitude of the state of Washington. Although a number of investigators have attributed these southern blade industries to 'northern influence', one of them has also remarked that this influence appears to exist only in the blade industry and not in additional elements of the artifact assemblage.

It seems reasonable to conclude, therefore, that Asian and Alaskan connections within the Palaeo-arctic tradition reflect a time in which Alaska was geographically a peninsula of Asia, thrusting against the continental ice of the New World; and that after about 7000 bc, with the final wasting of ice barriers, the technological vestiges of that tradition found in a variety of cultures of the American north-west were borne by hunters of the coast and of the interior, appearing as scattered and derivative industries that persisted as late as the Christian era.

CHAPTER III

People of the Spreading Forest

As the ice-caps melted and released their waters into the oceans at the close of the Wisconsin epoch, the broad tundra plain that had been Beringia was gradually encroached upon by rising sea levels. Around 8000 or 9000 bc, when the sea finally separated Asia from America, the intrusion of Pacific waters into the Arctic Ocean probably ameliorated the Alaskan climate. Until about 3000 bc, warming continued and the seas rose. In areas of North America that had been heavily laden with ice during the Wisconsin advances, the now unburdened land almost literally sprang upwards in isostatic adjustment, causing the level of the sea to appear to sink in relation to the land, even though the oceans as a whole continued to rise. Some of these reboundings were especially obvious in northern Canada, but most of Alaska north of the Alaska Peninsula, having borne little of the ice, was affected only slightly.

The climax of the post-glacial warming trend – the so-called Thermal Maximum – was apparently experienced throughout Arctic North America before 2000 bc, with the edge of the northern forest in some areas moving as much as 300 kilometres farther north than at present. A cooling trend was to follow around 1500 bc, with retreats of the forest edge and related vegetational changes.

By 4000 bc, there comes to be evident in Alaska – still at this date the only region of modern Eskimo territory to be completely occupied – a distinction between peoples oriented towards the coast and those confining themselves more to the interior. Although it might seem likely that the ancestry of the Eskimos and Aleuts lies with coastal people, the distinction between coastal and inland dwellers has remained blurred until quite recently, in particular because of the fact that there are sites and localities where artifacts of both appear. Consequently, a brief discussion of these apparent dwellers of the interior is necessary.

THE NORTHERN ARCHAIC TRADITION

Well-dated deposits from the site of Onion Portage have produced material that has been divided into two consecutive cultural complexes within a single technological tradition known as the Northern Archaic. The earliest materials, dated to about 4000 bc by several radiocarbon determinations, include somewhat asymmetrical projectile points with deep, wide, side-notches, and bases that are commonly rather convex; large unifacially chipped knives; and chipped endscrapers. As time goes on, some of the projectile points become shorter, the scraping implements

21　Locations mentioned in relation to the Northern Archaic tradition. Sites of the tradition occur in Yukon and Northwest Territories as well as in Alaska, where they are thought to represent influence emanating from interior North America to the south.

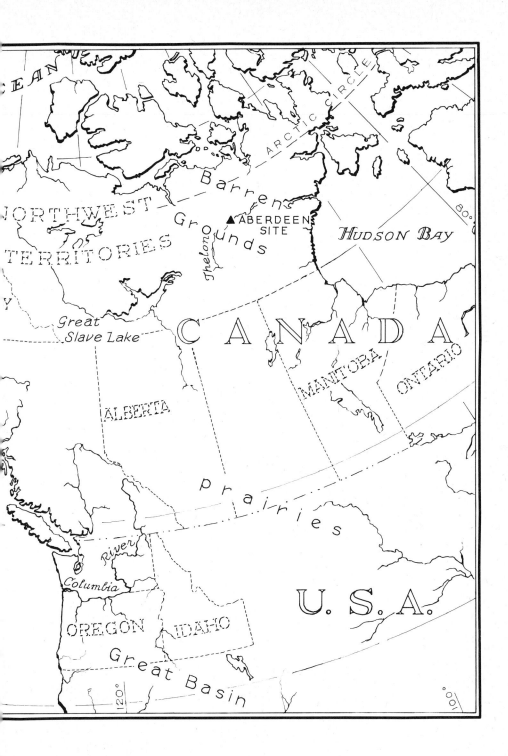

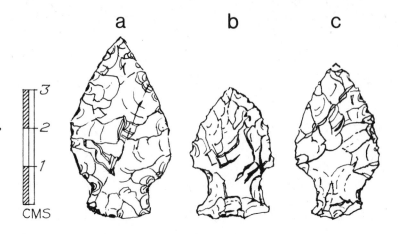

22 Northern Archaic tradition: projectile points: *a*, Palisades complex, Onion Portage; *b*, Ugashik Knoll phase, Ugashik River drainage; *c*, from a site near the mouth of the Kvichak River in south-western Alaska.

change slightly and notched pebbles, designed it seems to be hafted as axes, appear. Still later, the bases of the side-notched points tend to evolve into stems produced by corner-notching; notched water-worn pebbles develop, supposedly used as sinkers; and some slate objects with crudely polished or striated faces are found. So far, all these artifacts are aspects of what locally is termed the Palisades complex. By about 2600 bc lanceolate points are found together at Onion Portage with stemmed points, and the way is prepared for the development of the succeeding Portage complex of 2500 bc. All projectile points by this date are of generalized leaf, or lanceolate, form, but some other artifacts – cutting and scraping implements – continue without modification. Occupation of Onion Portage by people of the Portage complex and the Northern Archaic tradition ends about 2400 bc.

The original discovery of the Palisades complex took place in north-western Alaska, on the coastal bluffs behind Cape Krusenstern, where, however, it is thought to represent the incursion of a people more

22a

23

23 Northern Archaic tradition: projectile points of the Beachridge complex of the upper Naknek drainage, south-western Alaska, dating from about 2000 bc; length of the longer, 8 cm. This is a manifestation of the later aspect of the tradition such as is represented by the Portage complex of Onion Portage.

24 Northern Archaic tradition: front and top view of a core of Tuktu type from Healy Lake, Alaska; height, about 4.3 cm.

accurately described as being of the interior. Another site of the complex has been reported from the Noatak River in the same general region.

Related to the foregoing are a number of finds of the interior and of south-western Alaska, many of which are inadequately dated. Some assemblages apparently closely similar to those of the Palisades complex appear along the Yukon River downstream from the modern town of Circle, and at the Ratekin site near the modern Denali highway. Sites with projectile points that vary only slightly in form from Palisades points, and which occur with complexes generally similar to the Palisades, are also known in south-western Alaska. One such site is Security Cove, a coastal location apparently analogous to that of the bluffs behind Cape Krusenstern; a second is Kagati Lake on the Kanektok River some 160 kilometres inland from Security Cove.

The collections mentioned above seem not to be related to those of the earlier Palaeo-arctic tradition. Collections from certain other sites, however, do suggest the possibility of such a relationship. The Tuktu complex from an unstratified site at Anaktuvuk Pass, which is dated by a single radiocarbon determination to at least as early as 4000 bc, includes side-notched points virtually identical to those of the Palisades complex, as well as notched pebbles, some grinding of implements, similar endscrapers and also a lanceolate point form. Unlike Palisades, however, this complex contains numerous microblades apparently struck or pressed from cores which have been described as more 'tabular' than the Campus type. Although the Tuktu artifacts are from a surface deposit which could contain a mixture of objects from different periods, the association of Palisades-like projectile points with microblades apparently also occurs elsewhere.

Another deposit of the same complex is thought to exist at Healy Lake, in the zone between 10 and 15 centimetres from the surface, where 24 side-notched points and relatively broad microblades occur; there is no radiocarbon determination that relates directly to this level. Unfortunately, the site is so shallow – with three different components said to be present in the top 15 centimetres – that some archaeologists have hesitated to put complete faith in an apparent association confined to a single 5-centimetre excavation level. A similar conjunction of artifacts, however, is known from the Ugashik River on the Alaska Peninsula, where 22b plentiful projectile points are accompanied by scarce and rather broad microblades pressed from relatively crude cores, dating from about 3000 bc.

The Denali complex was mentioned in the preceding chapter, with some discussion of ambiguities in its dating. When originally defined, the complex was said to consist almost entirely of wedge-shaped microcores, the blades pressed from them, and of a certain class of burins, with some scattered side-notched points thought to be intrusive. But it was later redefined by other investigators. Based largely on evidence from Healy Lake and Dixthada in the Tanana uplands, and from Aishihik Lake in south-western Yukon Territory, the complex was broadened to include side-notched and stemmed projectile points, and to this newer

'Denali complex' was attributed a date later than that of Tuktu – from 2500 bc to as late as A D 1000. Such assemblages as these may be taken to relate to the Northern Archaic tradition, despite the fact that apparently very similar assemblages *without* the projectile points seem to be assignable to the much earlier Palaeo-arctic tradition.

As was indicated in the preceding chapter, other sites of importance in which side-notched projectile points occur with microblades have been reported to the east, in south-western Yukon Territory and in south-western Northwest Territories, where they may be as early as 3000 bc. In the former area, at least, it appears that microblades were not made after the beginning of the Christian era.

Thus, although some of the finds that include an apparent association of notched projectile points of the Northern Archaic tradition with microblades and microcores are from the surface or from sites so shallow that their evidence is less than absolutely compelling, and although it is clear that there are a number of sites in the Alaskan interior in which assemblages of the Archaic tradition do *not* include microblades, the evidence for the association of microblades and notched points in Alaska and western Canada seems convincing. Inasmuch as some of the microcores would be assigned to the wedge-shaped or Campus type, one must then accept that the so-called 'Denali complex' probably represents not one but two valid cultural entities: the first, of the Palaeo-arctic tradition, dating from as early as 8000 bc; the second, an aspect of the Northern Archaic tradition slightly different from that represented by the Palisades, Portage and Tuktu complexes.

All sites hitherto reported of the Northern Archaic tradition seem interpretable as temporary, seasonal camps, without permanent, con-structed habitations. In this they parallel the camps of the Palaeo-arctic tradition, with the one most likely exception of the coastal site at Anangula, mentioned in the preceding chapter.

The Northern Canadian Interior
The earliest dated complex in the area of Great Slave Lake, an assemblage termed the Acasta Lake complex of about 5000 bc, is characterized by chipped lanceolate point and knife forms in which stems or notches are only weakly developed. Well-defined side-notched projectile points appear in the later Oxbow complex of 2500 to 1500 bc. Sometime around 1000 bc the area was intruded upon for a period by a people usually found closer to the coast, people bearing the so-called Arctic Small Tool tradition, which will be discussed in a later chapter. Following that intrusion, and after about 200 bc, a considerable variety of stemmed and notched projectile points appear within various assemblages assigned to the Taltheilei Shale tradition, all of which are thought to represent ancestral Athapaskan Indians – specifically, the ancestors of the modern Yellow Knife Indians of the area.

Farther east, the sequence in the Barren Grounds between Great Slave Lake and Hudson Bay has been described on the basis of four consecutive cultural phases. The earliest of these, which includes lanceolate points, is said to show connections with the earlier big-game hunters of the more southerly, unglaciated part of North America, the Palaeo-Indians. The second phase apparently represents an intrusion from the Arctic coast of people of the Arctic Small Tool tradition. The third includes corner- and side-notched points and is taken to represent ancestral Athapaskans. The fourth and last represents another intrusion from the coast by the immediate ancestors of the Caribou Eskimos, who are the modern inhabitants.

This sequence seems to be generally confirmed by more recent excavations at the head of the Thelon River east of Great Slave Lake. Here again the earliest occupations were by people of a culture strongly reminiscent of that of the late Palaeo-Indians on the Great Plains to the south; these were followed by an incursion of Arctic Small Tool tradition people, and subsequently by the appearance of side-notched projectile points.

Still farther east, at the Aberdeen site near the mouth of the Thelon River, an assemblage characterized generally by lanceolate points comparable to the Palaeo-Indian Agate Basin type and which also includes side-notched projectile points not unlike those of the Northern Archaic tradition in Alaska, may be as late as 1100 bc. This assemblage is assigned by the excavator to what he has called the Shield Archaic tradition, a widespread cultural manifestation known from northern Manitoba and Ontario around the south of Hudson Bay, and which he has argued was a development from late Palaeo-Indian occupation to the south. This Shield Archaic occupation at Aberdeen seems to have preceded a weak incursion by people of the Arctic Small Tool tradition. After the beginning of the Christian era the area was inhabited by folk whose material culture was similar to that of the Taltheilei Shale tradition, and who are considered to have been the ancestors of the modern Athapaskan-speaking Chipewyan.

Summary and Comparisons

With regard to north-east Asia, it is fair to say simply that no parallels to the manifestations of the Northern Archaic tradition are known. The situation is quite different in America, however.

Implements not unlike the side- to corner-notched projectile points of the Palisades complex and its relatives were present from an early time in what is now southern Canada and the continental United States. In the east they occur in complexes of the Archaic stage apparently as early as 6000 bc. Farther west they appear in the southern prairies of Alberta possibly at a similar time. They are known in the Great Basin of inland western North America probably earlier than anywhere else on the continent, and appear in northern Idaho and along the middle Columbia River in Oregon before 5000 bc. Generally the assemblages in which these implements are found include heavy scrapers and other tools which suggest use by hunters of large game, and some are associated with bison, both extinct and modern species.

In the light of the foregoing, it seems fairly clear that the cultural complexes described in this chapter must have spread into the northern areas from the south, following the last deglaciation. Specifically, it is likely that people using lanceolate and side-notched stone projectile points moved north with the expansion of the northern forest during the warm weather of the Thermal Maximum, arriving in northern Canada and Alaska between 5000 and 4000 bc. In Alaska and western Canada the conjunction of some such implements with the microblades and microcores of the Palaeo-arctic tradition suggests some inter-ethnic social contact. Around 1000 bc, the Barren Grounds of central Canada were apparently abandoned by the descendants of these southern immigrants, only to be reoccupied around the beginning of the Christian era by culturally related people who have been considered by a number of investigators to be the ancestors of the modern Athapaskan Indian inhabitants of the area.

Thus the remains described in the preceding pages would seem to represent people of the American interior, who are unlikely to have been closely involved in the development of the later Eskimos and Aleuts. Nevertheless, the nature of their relationship to people of the earlier Palaeo-arctic tradition is evidently complicated, as is implied by the mixture of cultural traditions in the Tuktu complex and in the later aspect of the so-called 'Denali complex'.

CHAPTER IV

People of the Pacific Coast

Whether or not one views the Anangula site, mentioned earlier, as a settlement with a coastal economy, it is clear that at least by 4000 bc a pronounced adaptation to the sea coast had been achieved along the edges of the Pacific in the vicinity of Kodiak Island.

As indicated previously, this Pacific maritime region has some   25 marked differences in climate from the major part of the region inhabited by Eskimos. The cool summers and relatively warm winters, with generally open, unfrozen coastlines, contrast strongly with the coastal ice-packs farther north. In the Aleutian zone, normal daily temperatures vary from a low in winter of around 20 degrees Fahrenheit to a summer high of about 60, and weather is frequently foggy. As one moves up the coast to the north-east, along the southern side of the Alaska Peninsula and around Kodiak Island, greater extremes of summer warmth and winter cold are experienced, but freezing of the sea coast is still confined only to the deeper, fjorded inlets near the mouths of freshwater streams, until one penetrates Cook Inlet as far as modern Anchorage. Rainfall in most of the coastal zone varies from around 750 to more than 2500 millimetres, with 1500 millimetres being fairly common. In this ice-free maritime region open-sea-hunting techniques were used by native peoples all the year round in pursuit of resident sea otter, hair seal and sea lion, and seasonally in search of migrating fur seals and whales. Walruses were seen only rarely. Whales, great and small, were especially abundant in the area from Unimak Island eastwards to Kodiak, as were fur seals and other resident sea mammals, and it was here that the major native human population was found. Despite the relative uniformity of the ecosystem, however, this population fell into two major linguistic divisions, Aleutian and Eskimoan, with the dividing line between them on the Pacific coast of the Alaska Peninsula somewhere near 159 degrees west longitude, at least by the nineteenth century.

There are good precedents for considering both Aleuts and Pacific Eskimos as a single southern unit, belonging together despite their linguistic differences, and despite gross distinctions that might be made in some aspects of material culture. Within their relatively uniform ecological zone, the two peoples shared a great number of subsistence techniques and made use of items of equipment that within the framework of all Eskimos and Aleuts are distinctly southern – items such as the two-holed kayak and, in place of the toggling harpoons used for large sea mammals by other Eskimos, a multi-barbed harpoon dart head. This sharing extends broadly throughout the kits of bone and

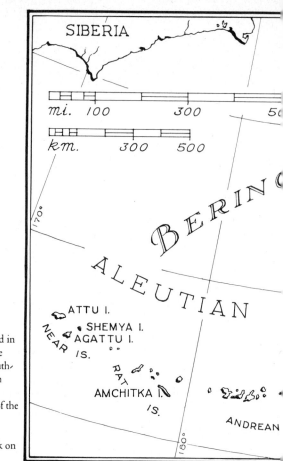

25 Locations mentioned in relation to traditions of the Pacific coastal zone of south-western Alaska. Through much of prehistory the boundary between areas of the Kodiak and Aleutian traditions apparently lay somewhat east of Chignik on the Alaska Peninsula.

antler tools. One quantitative study of bone and antler artifacts, for instance, reveals that the assemblages of both Aleuts and Pacific Eskimos cluster together in mutual distinction from those known farther north in Alaska, and concludes that it is scarcely possible to distinguish the Aleut and Pacific Eskimo areas on the basis of whole collections of bone artifacts alone. This is not the case with stone tools, however, as will be shown.

In this chapter, the archaeological remains of periods after 4000 bc will be summarized by means of three major traditions. Although these traditions are defined on relatively the same level of abstraction as are those commonly distinguished in the Eskimo zone of the north, units of precisely this scale have seldom been used for the people of the Pacific – those chosen heretofore having been either broader and more summary, or narrower and more detailed.

THE OCEAN BAY TRADITION

Materials assigned to the Ocean Bay tradition are found in the Kodiak Island region of the zone occupied by Pacific Eskimos, and probably also in the Aleutian Islands.

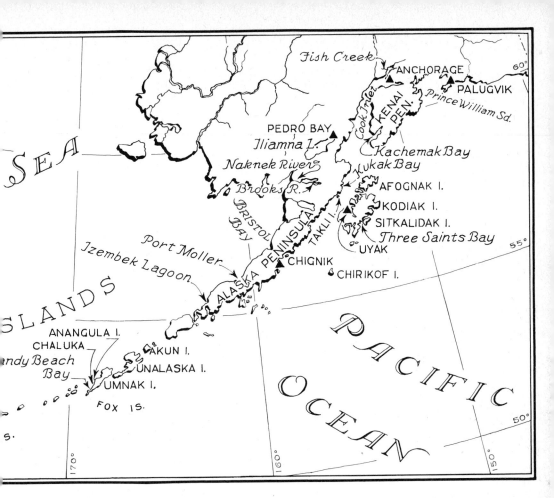

In the Kodiak region, the complexes included are those designated·
Ocean Bay I from the Ocean Bay site on Sitkalidak Island off the south-
east coast of Kodiak Island proper; a related complex from site Afo-106
at the mouth of the Afognak River on southern Afognak Island of the
Kodiak group; and components of the Takli Alder phase known from
three sites – two on Takli Island and one at Kukak Bay – along the coast
of the Alaska Peninsula. These complexes have been dated by
radiocarbon to between 3900 and 3500 bc.

Among stone artifacts all the collections include large numbers of
leaf-shaped, percussion-flaked knives or heavy projectile heads; relatively long and narrow percussion-flaked knives or projectile blades
with weakly developed, tapering stems; and a variety of scrapers. One of
the sites yielded some better-made projectile blades, often of chert, with
relatively long stems that are triangular in cross-section, as well as a few
gouge-like adze blades with polished bits. A single stone vessel that was
apparently used as a lamp, presumably to burn sea-mammal oil, has
been found. The lowest levels of the Afognak River site yielded fairly
conclusive evidence of a microblade industry; one site on Takli Island
yielded occasional blades, but not conclusive evidence of the presence of
an important blade industry.

26

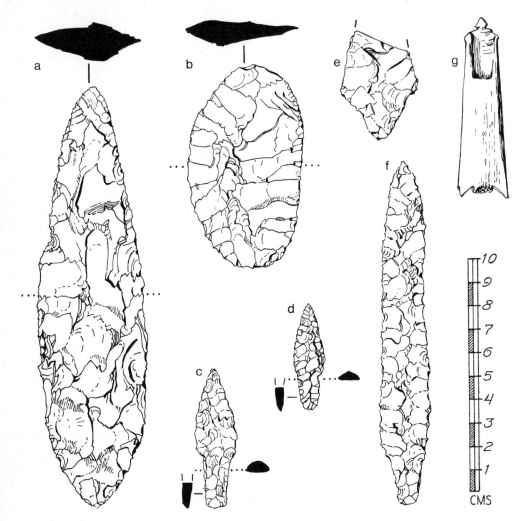

a   b   e   g

f

d

c

10
9
8
7
6
5
4
3
2
1
CMS

26   Ocean Bay tradition, Takli Alder phase: stone and bone implements from Takli Island: *a, b*, large chipped bifaces; *c–f*, chipped-stone projectile or lance points; *g*, fragment of barbed bone harpoon head with an open bed at the tip, probably to receive the base of a stone point such as *c* or *d*, which has a stem with a rather triangular cross-section and a markedly bevelled butt.

Barbed bone harpoon dart heads, of the general class so characteristic of the Pacific coastal zone at all times, were in use, although they are poorly represented in the collections, in which relatively little organic material is preserved. Unlike most later examples of the same basic implement, provision for the attachment of the harpoon line was by means of a heavy projection, rather than of a cut or drilled hole.

The only site at which bone waste was recovered produced remains of sea otter, seal, sea lion, porpoise, and larger whales. Its location on an islet off the Pacific coast of the Alaska Peninsula makes it likely that a major endeavour of its inhabitants was the taking of sea mammals. On the other hand, the location of another site near the mouth of the Afognak River, an area considerably inland from the open coast where ice forms during the winter, suggests that it may rather have been placed to take advantage of summer runs of migrating salmon.

The only possible evidence for a dwelling so far discovered is an arc of four post-holes encountered in a trench at one of the two Takli Island sites which, if the remains of a shelter, would indicate an ellipsoidal or round structure about 8 metres in diameter. Despite this near-absence of evidence for habitations, the quantity of artifacts and debris at both Takli Island sites suggest relatively permanent occupation at least of these coastal stations.

In the Aleutian Islands, evidence for the presence of the Ocean Bay tradition is still ambiguous, and some investigators reject the possibility that its presence will ever be clearly demonstrated. Nevertheless, a presumed sea-mammal projectile blade of chipped stone, from levels dated about 1750 bc in a site on Islelo, an islet off the coast of Akun Island in the eastern Aleutians, has been compared to material from the Ocean Bay tradition on Takli Island. To the latter may also be compared collections of elongated, chipped projectile blades from the site at Sandy Beach Bay on Umnak Island, dating from between 3000 and 2000 bc, as well as similar implements from a location near the Anangula blade site on an islet off the shore of Umnak Island, where they date from about 4000 bc.

The Ocean Bay collection from Takli Island has also been compared with a collection from the Near Islands in the far-western Aleutians, which is dated to about the beginning of the Christian era or perhaps to the first millennium bc. In view of certain similarities noted it has been hypothesized that a recognizable archaeological horizon embracing the combined Pacific Eskimo and Aleut regions will be found dating from about 4000 bc, indicating a time of ethnic unity of ancestral peoples of the Pacific. At present, however, the existence of a horizon so widespread as this is not certain.

To sum up, the Ocean Bay tradition includes materials of a clearly evident archaeological horizon of the Pacific Eskimo region of the fourth millennium bc, which may well have had its origins in some earlier tradition within which blade-making was important. The presence of the Ocean Bay tradition in the Kodiak region is unmistakable; within the Aleutian Islands it seems probable, although it has not been fully demonstrated.

THE KODIAK TRADITION

The Kodiak tradition is the term used here to refer to all archaeological remains of ground-slate-using people of the Eskaleut Pacific zone before about AD 1000; it is divisible into two main stages. The technological dimensions are sufficiently limited that the notion of a single great tradition seems defensible, despite the fact that during a period of some three-and-a-half millennia a number of distinct periods and several local subtraditions are distinguishable. Throughout, the technology was based upon the production of polished slate implements of a variety of forms and functions; upon the use of an extensive inventory of bone tools, the forms of a number of which were foreshadowed in collections of the Ocean Bay tradition; upon the employment of the oil lamp; upon the hunting of sea mammals; and upon the subsidiary, but often

27 Kodiak tradition, Takli stage: pecked stone lamp (repaired), Brooks River Strand phase, upper Naknek drainage, Alaska Peninsula; maximum width, 20.2 cm; depth of bowl, 1.6 cm.

27

28 Implements of the Kodiak tradition: *a*, chipped stone point of the Takli stage, betraying a relationship with the earlier Ocean Bay tradition; *b*, *c*, polished slate dart or lance blades, Takli stage; *d*, *e*, bone harpoon dart heads of Kachemak and Takli stages respectively, the latter with an open bed in which would be affixed a stone point, and a lateral guard rather than a hole to secure the harpoon line; all from Alaska Peninsula.

enormously important, use of fish, especially the migrating salmon. Unlike the earlier Ocean Bay tradition, collections that may reasonably be assigned to the Kodiak tradition do not extend significantly into the zone of occupation by ethnographically known Aleuts.

The earliest complexes are here known as the Takli stage of the tradition. These include those designated Ocean Bay II from Sitkalidak Island and from site Afo-109 near the mouth of the Afognak River; the earliest prehistoric component at Pedro Bay on the north-east portion of Iliamna Lake; the earliest part of collections assigned to the Takli Birch phase from three sites along the Pacific coast of the Alaska Peninsula; elements of what has been designated the Brooks River Strand phase of the upper Naknek River drainage on the Alaska Peninsula; and the Old Islanders complex of Chirikof Island. These early complexes are characterized by long thrusting implements of polished slate, usually but not always manufactured by extensive sawing and scraping of the slate; by the use of the oil lamp; and by the use of implements of chipped stone, highly reminiscent of those of the earlier Ocean Bay tradition and which vary substantially in frequency from site to site. None of the collections have the later, highly characteristic transverse knife of polished slate, the *ulu*. Their radiocarbon dates all fall within the period 2500 to 1900 bc.

The nature of the sites varies. The original Ocean Bay site, the three sites on or near the Pacific Coast of the Alaska Peninsula and the Old Islanders site on Chirikof Island must have been located with a view towards the taking of sea mammals. The Afognak site was apparently located for the purpose of seasonal fishing. The small camp-sites excavated at the mouth of the Brooks River in the upper Naknek drainage included quantities of smashed scraps of mammal longbone

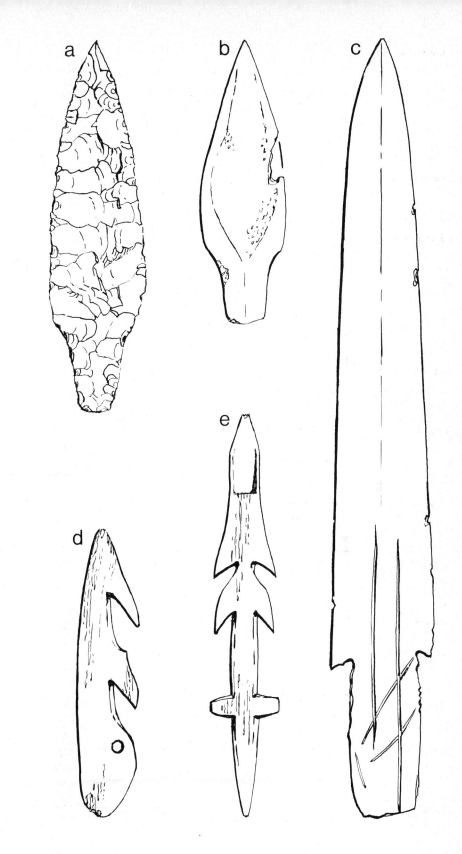

a

b

c

e

d

5
4
3
2
1
CMS

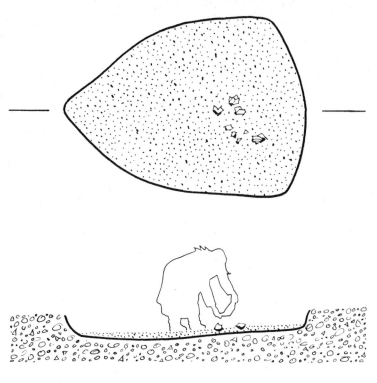

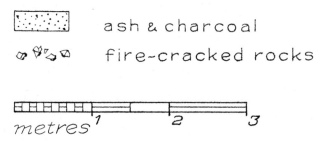

29   Kodiak tradition, Takli
stage: plan of a dwelling –
presumably a tent – of the
Brooks River Strand phase,
upper Naknek drainage;
charcoal from the floor was
radiocarbon dated to about
2500 bc.

presumed to be from caribou, and one included a very decayed fragment
probably of caribou skull. The purpose of the Pedro Bay occupation
could be either land-mammal hunting or fishing, probably the former.

The evidence for habitations is confined to post-holes that possibly
outlined a round or ellipsoidal structure some 7 by 5 metres in size, with
no internal fire or indication of an entrance, of the early Takli Birch
phase on Takli Island, and to a tear-drop-shaped dwelling of the Strand

29   phase at the mouth of the Brooks River; the latter is interpreted as the
floor of a temporary structure, possibly a tent.

In view of the positions of the sites, and of the nature of the chipped
stone represented in most of them, the earliest people of the Kodiak
tradition seem to have been descended almost directly from their
predecessors of the Ocean Bay tradition. They have, however, added the
technique for working slate by sawing and polishing, and they appear to
have expanded their subsistence base to include the hunting of land

mammals, although it would be most unwise to conclude on the basis of present evidence that their predecessors did not also engage in this. Undoubtedly indicative of their continued primary focus upon the coast, however, is that the two inland sites of the Alaska Peninsula in which their remains have been found are located at the extreme upper ends of the Bering Sea drainage systems, where they are nearest to the Pacific coast, and that in the Brooks River vicinity they had transported oil burning lamps to their hunting camp.

The later complexes of the Kodiak tradition are here called the Kachemak stage. These include collections from Kodiak Island known as Old Kiavak and Three Saints, and the closely related assemblages of Kachemak Bay on the Kenai Peninsula and of the lower levels of the Uyak site on Kodiak Island, which together have been seen as belonging to what one writer has termed a 'Kachemak tradition', and date variously from the period 1500 bc to AD 1000. For present purposes, to these can be added the later elements of the collections from sites along the Pacific coast of the Alaska Peninsula that have been assigned to the Takli Birch phase, and which date from about 1500 to 1000 bc, as well as a single later assemblage from the same vicinity, designated the Takli Cottonwood phase, which dates from just after the beginning of the Christian era. The Kachemak stage as a whole seems to cover the period from 1500 bc to AD 1000.

Broadly speaking, all these assemblages include a great variety of implements of polished slate which before grinding were shaped first by chipping, rather than by initial sawing, and which include the transverse ulu as well as other knives and projectile blades. Also plentiful are oil *30* lamps of stone, some of them highly decorated; labrets of stone or bone; and a great variety of bone implements, including now some toggling harpoon heads – designed to twist in the wound in order to hold firm – as well as the more common barbed-harpoon dart head. Both slate knife and lance blades and bone harpoon dart heads have drilled holes for attachment for the first time.

30 Kodiak tradition, Kachemak stage: polished-slate ulu, Takli Island, near Alaska Peninsula; maximum present width, 11.7 cm.

31 Kodiak tradition, Kachemak stage: decorated stone lamp of the Takli Cottonwood phase, from Takli Island, near the Alaska Peninsula; length, 26 cm. The paired bulges in the bowl have been interpreted – without any evidence other than purely visual – as a woman's breasts.

In the elements mentioned, the material culture of the Kachemak stage partook of a tendency toward an increase in the variety both of polished stone tools and of bone implements for sea-mammal hunting. This tendency was manifest all along the north-western coast of North America to the south, appearing in the early second millennium bc in British Columbia, and eventually involving the entire intervening coast.

By the last millennium bc, increasing differentiation of peoples in local areas within what is now the Eskimo zone of the Pacific coast was of a degree sufficient to mask some of the signs of continuity with the preceding Takli stage of the Kodiak tradition, much more so with the still earlier Ocean Bay tradition. Nevertheless, in the collections that compose the Takli Birch phase this continuity is clearly represented, while numerous specific artifactual attributes are shared with collections from Kachemak Bay and from the Uyak site on Kodiak Island. In turn, the Uyak and Kachemak Bay collections reflect a number of specific artifact similarities with the collections of Old Kiavak and Three Saints Bay on Kodiak. These latter, however, show considerably fewer links with collections from the Takli Birch phase.

By about the beginning of the Christian era, other manifestations of the Kachemak stage of the Kodiak tradition appear in Prince William Sound, especially at the important site of Palugvik. And there is evidence later in the millennium of at least the seasonal presence of people of this tradition at a site on Fish Creek at the extreme upper end of Cook Inlet. By this time, however, sites along the Alaska Peninsula are beginning to show signs of a divergence from the rest of the Pacific zone, apparently as the result of influence from contemporary people of the Bering Sea slope. Nevertheless, during the Kachemak stage the degree of similarity and of technological continuity throughout the zone are here taken to mean that variations are due to time and distance, not to the presence of any strict social barriers to communications such as might indicate the existence of different ethnic groups.

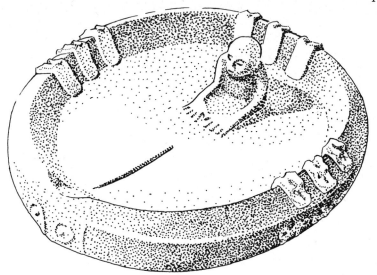

32 Kodiak tradition, Kachemak stage: pecked and polished-stone lamp from Fish Creek on upper Cook Inlet; length, 32 cm. Such decorated lamps appear to date from the first millennium AD.

Most sites excavated have yielded considerable midden deposits, and with them abundant evidence of a primary orientation towards sea-mammal hunting, with fishing as an important secondary source of supply. In these middens, excavations of houses have often been extremely difficult, but it is clear from cuts in sites throughout the zone that the dwellings were predominantly semi-subterranean, at least sometimes square, and might have a central hearth. There is little or no information regarding entrances.

As the Kodiak tradition developed through the Kachemak stage, material culture became progressively more elaborate until the first millennium AD, when a high point was reached in the finish of artifacts, in the presence of numerous items of personal adornment such as beads and labrets, in the engraving of designs on implement points of ground slate, and especially in the development of heavy lamps of pecked stone which might contain devices rising from the interior of the oil bowl – devices such as human or animal figures, or what are apparently human female breasts. Since a large number of sites have been found, most of which have yielded an abundance of material, it may be assumed that the human population was relatively dense at this time.

By about AD 500, influences from the Bering Sea were strong enough for at least one site, at Kukak Bay on the Alaska Peninsula, to represent possibly a permanent village of such outsiders, although the similarity of a number of the implements to indigenous types makes it possible that the foreign presence was not quite so extreme, and that the village included at least a significant proportion of Pacific coastal natives. At any rate, the changes in the tool assemblage, with a very marked increase in the chipping of small projectile points of chert, are drastic enough to warrant the separation of collections of this phase – the Kukak Beach phase – from the Kachemak tradition proper. Although a similar influence towards the production of small chipped implements had already appeared in the foregoing Takli Cottonwood phase, evidence for continuity with other sites of the Kodiak tradition is strong enough to cause the single site known for that phase to be presumed to represent a Pacific coastal group under relatively slight foreign influence. In the Beach phase a few houses also appear that are square, probably entered by a sloping entrance passageway; they seem large enough to have served as a kind of men's house or ceremonial house like the similar structures known from later Eskimo sites. The only one of these to be fully excavated yielded an unusually high proportion of small projectile points in relation to ulus and other domestic implements, leading to the conclusion that it might, indeed, have been a residence predominantly for men.

By about this same time, the end of the first millennium A D, there occur on Kodiak other innovations – such as the grooved stone-splitting adze and the vapour sweat bath – which may have derived not from the Bering Sea, but rather from people of the coast to the east and south of the Pacific Eskimo zone. Together with the influences from the Bering Sea, these introductions contributed to the culture of the historical Eskimo-speaking Koniag of Kodiak and the surrounding areas, as it is known both archaeologically and ethnographically after A D 1000. We will return to the Koniag in a later chapter.

With its roots in the earlier Ocean Bay tradition, then, the Kodiak tradition was characterized by an increasing use of polished-slate implements among coastal dwellers of the general Kodiak region, who, through time, manifested more and more regional diversity. The earliest or Takli stage of development saw the construction and use of long knives or thrusting implements of slate, although in some subareas chipped knives and projectile heads also retained popularity. After about 1500 bc, with the Kachemak stage of the tradition, an increasing range of implements were made by polishing, including the transverse knife or ulu. The tradition reached a zenith during the first millennium A D, with the production of decorated lamps of stone and of numerous items of personal adornment. By this time, however, the Kachemak stage people on the Pacific coast of the Alaska Peninsula were experiencing pressure from their Bering Sea contemporaries to the north and west.

Although it is likely that the earlier Ocean Bay tradition was represented within the area later inhabited by the historical Aleuts, it is clear that bearers of the Kodiak tradition never extended west of the zone inhabited at the time of European contact by so-called Pacific Eskimos.

THE ALEUTIAN TRADITION

The tradition here called Aleutian will embrace all those artifact assemblages found in the zone west of the slate-polishers of the Kodiak tradition and dating from after about 3000 bc. In the east, this zone includes the Port Moller and Chignik region of the Alaska Peninsula. Although it is possible that some of the people of the Alaska Peninsula thus included were not in fact the direct ancestors of linguistic Aleuts of later times (inasmuch as the precise location of the boundary between

Aleuts and Eskimos on the Peninsula has not been settled), the weight of present evidence suggests that they were.

Throughout the territory and time-period of the Aleutian tradition stone tool assemblages are dominated by chipped implements, many of which are stemmed points and knives of various forms, while polished slate appears only relatively late – at the end of the first millennium A D – and then is confined in many sites to the common transverse knife or ulu. In these respects, the collections of Aleutian tradition betray their greatest differences from those of the Kodiak tradition. On the other hand, the oil lamp appears throughout, as it does in the Kodiak zone, and the bone-tool types are very similar to those in use by people of the Kodiak tradition.

33, 34

As was the case to the east, middens in the Aleutian zone contain large quantities of sea-mammal bones, which vary from site to site in the proportions in which they appear relative to the other major components, such as the remains of invertebrates, especially the sea urchin; of fish, especially marine fish such as cod, halibut, sculpin, and greenling; and of bird, both migratory and resident. Generally speaking, migratory animals – that is, fur seals and whales – are more common in the eastern portion of Aleutian territory. On the Alaska Peninsula and the easternmost islands caribou and, occasionally, bear add to the midden debris. Farther out in the island chain native land mammals are represented chiefly by foxes and, since the arrival of Europeans, rats.

Archaeological remains from the zone will be described by area, moving east to west.

The Alaska Peninsula and the Eastern Fox Islands

Excavations at the Hot Springs site at Port Moller, on the Alaska Peninsula, have produced a largely unpublished collection of artifacts from a lengthy occupation that begins by 1500 bc, according to the radiocarbon evidence, and ends sometime before the coming of Europeans. The site consists both of midden areas and of some 250 depressions believed to represent prehistoric houses.

Stone artifacts are dominated by chipped implements, including some stemmed asymmetrical knives reminiscent of objects from the Aleutian Islands, and chipped projectile blades reminiscent of objects both from the eastern Aleutian Islands and from sites within the area of Eskimo occupation on the Bering Sea. Polished-stone implements are virtually non-existent. Bone artifacts are represented especially by harpoon dart heads, but include other projectile heads, fish spears and awls.

Two houses were found to be elliptical in plan, excavated about 50 centimetres into the contemporary ground surface, about 4–5 metres across in their maximum dimension, and with no visible entry, suggesting that they were entered through the roof. Radiocarbon determinations indicate that the houses date from about A D 500 and A D 1300 respectively. A third, larger house was more nearly rectangular, with rounded corners, about 7.5 by 12.5 metres in size and, again, was

35

Objects illustrating
similarities between the
Aleutian and Kodiak
traditions.

33   Carved ivory objects;
left and right, Kachemak
stage of the Kodiak tradition,
Kodiak Island; centre,
Aleutian tradition, seal or sea
lion linked ornament,
Unalaska, Fox Islands,
Aleutians; length of item on
the left, 7.5 cm.

34   Harpoon dart heads of
bone; left, Takli stage of the
Kodiak tradition, Takli
Island, near Alaska
Peninsula; right, Aleutian
tradition, Umnak, western
Fox Islands; length of item on
the left, 9.7 cm.

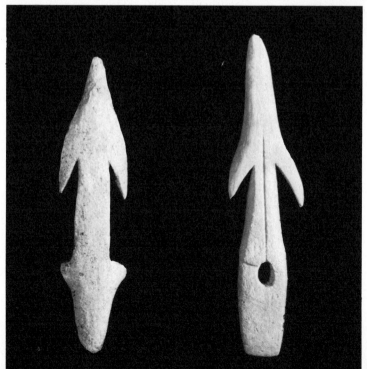

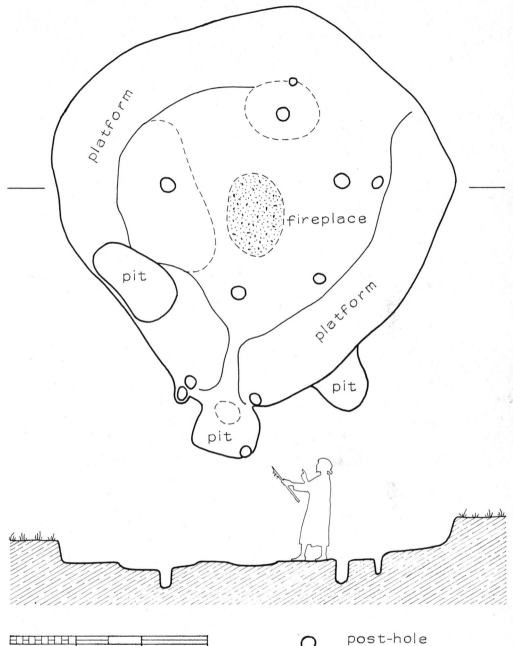

platform

platform

fireplace

pit

pit

pit

metres 1 2 3

○ post-hole

◌ shallow depression

35 Aleutian tradition, Alaska Peninsula: plan and section of a house at Port Moller, radiocarbon dated to about AD 1300. The roof was probably of driftwood and sod.

excavated into the contemporary surface and had no visible entrance; this house had a radiocarbon date of around AD 500.

Similar artifact assemblages appear to be present north-eastwards up the Peninsula at least as far as the Chignik area, a point slightly east of the Eskimo-Aleut boundary of historical times.

36

South-west of Port Moller, at Izembek Lagoon, excavations have produced a semi-subterranean house constructed with boulder walls and a framework of whale mandibles, elliptical in plan and with a central hearth; external dimensions were about 8 by 9 metres; there was no visible entry. The artifacts recovered included, on the one hand, chipped-stone implements strongly reminiscent of those from Port Moller, and, on the other, implements of polished slate strikingly similar to those known around Bristol Bay at AD 1000 and after (to be discussed later). Radiocarbon determinations from the house and related deposits suggest a date of about AD 1000 for the house and the artifact assemblage. Preservation of bone artifacts was poor.

Still farther to the south-west, excavations in Chulka midden on Akun Island revealed an assemblage of which about one-third of the implements were of polished slate, including ulus. One radiocarbon determination would suggest a date as early as AD 800, while others fall within the second millennium. Excavations nearby indicate clearly that earlier deposits were without polished-slate implements. As mentioned before, one of these sites yielded at least one artifact that has been compared to the elongated, chipped projectile heads characteristic of collections of the earlier Ocean Bay tradition.

The research which has been carried out along the Alaska Peninsula and in the Eastern Fox Islands is not adequate enough for us to be able to give a firm picture of cultural relationships. Nevertheless it is tempting to think that a relatively uniform culture employing chipped-stone artifacts and the usual harpoon dart heads of bone existed in the area until about the end of the first millennium AD, when to it was added a technology involving the polishing both of transverse knives and of projectile points of slate. Such a view requires, of course, that the latest radiocarbon date from Port Moller (AD 1300), derived from a house in which no slate implements were found, be considered erroneous.

The Western Fox Islands

Large numbers of artifacts were recovered on Unalaska Island by American military men during World War II, but even though many of the larger collections have now come to public museums, no complete descriptions have ever been published. Sites are reportedly plentiful. On Unalaska Island in particular these may include depressions resulting from large, communal, semi-subterranean houses some 6 metres or so in width and 20 metres or more in length, such as were inhabited at the time of, or at any rate not long after, the arrival of the Russians. Somewhat more information is available from extensive scientific excavations on Umnak Island, in the so-called Chaluka midden at Nikolski village, although these too have been only incompletely reported.

36　Aleutian tradition, Alaska Peninsula: chipped-stone blades, left to right, two lance or projectile blades, a sideblade and a polished adze blade, all from the Chignik region; length of sideblade, 5 cm.

At Chaluka, as in other areas of the Aleutians, the stone industries are characterized by the technique of chipping, with polished-stone implements appearing only very late, except that pecked- and polished-stone lamps occur throughout. The periods known as Early and Middle Chaluka together last from about 2000 to 1000 bc. Stone implements in both are predominantly unifacial, but also include numerous small, fine, bifacially chipped projectile points. In the earliest period, although not in the lowest levels, stemmed knives of chipped stone were found, often with asymmetrical blades. Although no excavated houses have been published, they seem to have been made of large round stones and whalebones, and in part were paved with flat, angular stone slabs; they were possibly 4–5 metres across; and small square or rectangular fire pits were formed of upright stone slabs.

Upper Chaluka is apparently separated by at least a thousand years from Middle Chaluka, beginning sometime in the first millennium A D. At this time the stone industry was predominantly bifacial, with a number of large, thick knives, and stemmed knives with asymmetrical blades; also common are stone chisels and large, flat, two-notched sinkers. It was only late in this period – certainly after A D 1000 and perhaps after A D 1500 – that artifacts of polished slate began to appear among the chipped implements.

Throughout all periods the bone industry includes a large number of harpoon dart heads, both bilaterally and unilaterally barbed, as well as barbed implements without line attachments that have been called spears. Although the styles of these projectile heads vary throughout the periods, their general form is constant. They are accompanied also by various wedges, awls, and tools thought to be root-diggers, beamers, and prying tools. Ornaments, including labrets, also appear throughout. *38–43* The bone waste shows exactly what might be expected from the insular location of the site: although there were fluctuations probably represent-ing some changes through time in preferences for specific animals, the

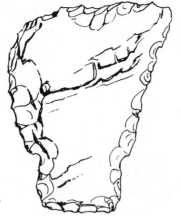

CMS

37 Aleutian tradition, Umnak, Fox Islands: chipped-stone knives.

38–43 Objects of the Aleutian tradition, Umnak, Fox Islands: top to bottom: ivory figure (height, 6 cm); portion of a bone dart head with complicated barbs (length, 14.4 cm); two ivory pins, one with a double face at one end (length, 15.6 cm); bone dart head or foreshaft (length, 16.9 cm); and ivory labret or lip-plug (width at widest point, 5 cm).

people were always clearly oriented towards the sea, taking large numbers of hair and fur seals, sea lions, and sea otter, as well as some whales and numerous fish.

37   Excavations in a site on Sandy Beach Bay, Umnak Island, have revealed an occupation with some similarity to that represented by Early Chaluka, and which radiocarbon determinations suggest began by 3000 bc. Houses were elliptical, about 3 by 5 metres in size, and were it seems entered from the roof. Reportedly, the small collection of stone artifacts includes a high proportion of relatively long and slender chipped projectile blades, resembling in this way assemblages both from the Takli Alder phase, mentioned earlier, and from the Near Islands, to be discussed shortly.

The Rat Islands

The most complete reports of excavations anywhere in the Aleutians are those dealing with Amchitka Island. Both stone and bone artifacts are in a general way similar to those from the Chaluka midden, representing a sequence that begins around 1000 bc. Unlike the Chaluka collections, however, those from Amchitka do not indicate a shift from pre-dominantly unifacial stone tools to predominantly bifacial ones. Indeed, higher proportions of bifacially formed implements are from lower levels on Amchitka, suggesting, if anything, a trend towards unifacial implements later in time.

The substantial sample of faunal waste includes sea mammals, birds, fish, and marine invertebrates. The sea mammals consist chiefly of sea otter and hair seal, both of which are year-round residents of the area, with fewer sea lions and migratory fur seals, and with still fewer whales, although both large and small whales are represented. Fish are ocean varieties, predominantly those to be found close inshore; no freshwater fish (salmon and char both occur today on the island during the spawning season) were identified, although this may be the result simply of the lesser chances of survival of their soft bones. Birds include cormorants, ducks, geese and swans, and smaller numbers of gulls,

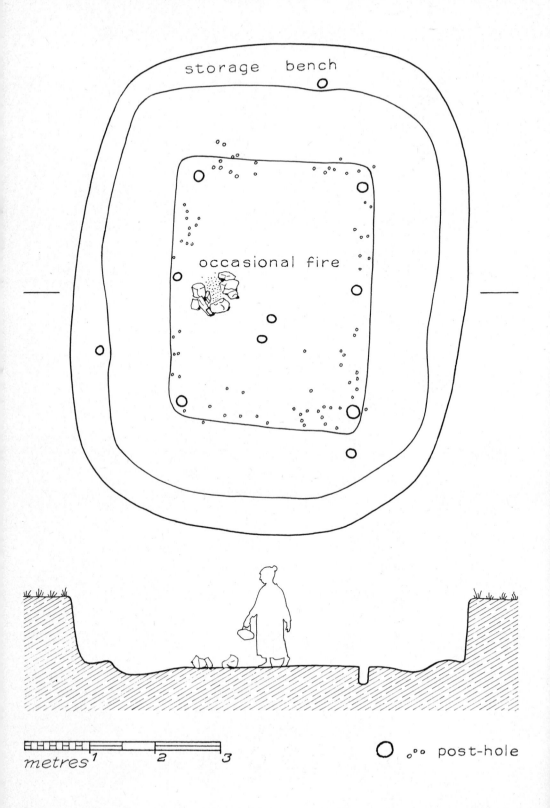

storage bench

occasional fire

metres 1 2 3

○ ₀°₀ post-hole

albatrosses and other birds. Invertebrates comprise sea urchins especially, followed in popularity by limpets, while other shellfish, including mussels, were present in much less substantial quantities.

A house dating from about AD 1500 was sub-rectangular, about 5 by 6 metres in size, excavated somewhat below the contemporary ground surface into bedrock, and was presumably entered from a hole in the roof. A crescent shaped hearth in the floor had apparently been seldom used. Associated tools include polished-stone ulus which were thought to represent the earliest polished slate at the site.

The Near Islands

Still farther to the west and forming the tip of the Aleutian Islands chain, the Near Islands appear to be stylistically the least typical of the Aleutians. The most complete published description is of a collection excavated at Krugloi Point on Agattu Island, which is supplemented by descriptive information regarding scattered materials from Agattu, Attu, and Shemya. Radiocarbon evidence suggests an occupation of these islands as early as about 600 bc.

The predominantly chipped-stone artifacts include an unusually high proportion of elliptical to leaf-shaped bifaces, some of which may have

44 Aleutian tradition, Amchitka, Rat Islands: plan and section of a house, radiocarbon dated to about AD 1500. The small posts or poles that surrounded the centre section are thought to have supported mats partitioning off the slightly depressed sitting and sleeping area that occupied the periphery of the interior of the house (see Ill. 10). The roof was of driftwood and sod.

45 Aleutian tradition, Agattu, Near Islands: chipped-stone artifacts dating from about the beginning of the Christian era: *a, b*, large bifaces; *c–f*, projectile or lance points.

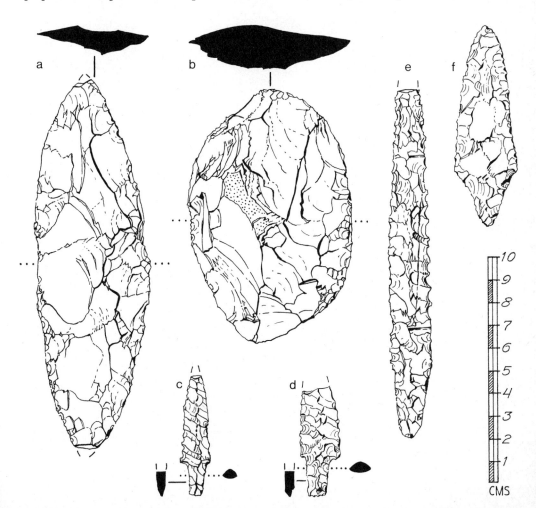

CMS

served as large projectile heads, as well as long and relatively slender points, often with well-developed stems, some of which are triangular in cross-section. Absent entirely are the asymmetrical stemmed knives that are common elsewhere in the islands. It is this apparent divergence from the usual Aleutian pattern that led one investigator, as mentioned earlier, to compare the Near Islands assemblages to those known much earlier from the Ocean Bay tradition of the Kodiak region, and to suggest that the Near Islands artifacts somehow represent in their divergence the survival of a much earlier tradition. Since that comparison was made, other comparable materials have been reported from the Islelo site near Akun Island, and from the Sandy Beach Bay and Anangula sites on Umnak Island, as was indicated in the discussion of the Ocean Bay tradition.

46 Aleutian tradition, Agattu, Near Islands: bone harpoon dart heads, the two at left with projections to hold the line; length of the longest, 22.5 cm.

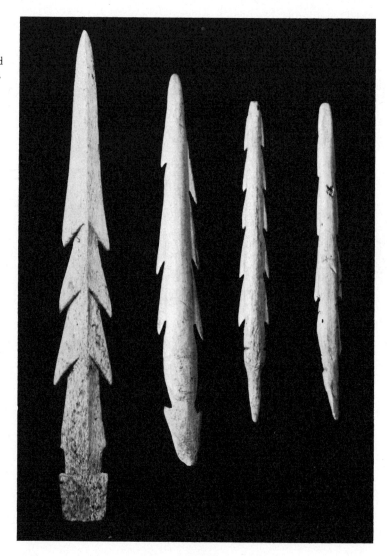

Despite this Near Island distinctiveness among recent stone artifacts, however, the bone implements include classes found in most of the other recent prehistoric Aleut sites, although with certain local stylistic differences. The polished-slate ulu appeared only very late in the sequence, perhaps no earlier than the arrival of the Russians in the eighteenth century.

46

The Aleutian Tradition: Origin and Change

It is clear that people directly ancestral to modern Aleuts were occupying the Fox Island group as early as or not long after 3000 bc, the Rat Island group as early as 1000 bc and the Near Island group as early as 600 bc. Throughout recent millennia these people developed local specializations in tool forms within their basic traditions of stone chipping and the use of harpoon dart heads of bone. There is no evidence of any kind to suggest that they or their immediate forbears populated the Aleutian Islands from the west, directly from Asia, and many researchers now believe not only that Aleut colonization came from the east, but that it occurred over a period of time not much earlier than that represented by the dated occupations just mentioned. However, the geomorphologically based argument that the 8000-year-old blade site at Anangula (see chapter II) indicates people already able to travel by boat, implies that the initial occupation of islands farther west in the Aleutians could well have occurred several millennia earlier than the dates so far known in most of the chain, although the relationship of the historically known Aleuts to any predecessors earlier than 3000 bc is the subject of disagreement.

Despite suggestions that traces of the Ocean Bay tradition of about 4000 bc may be found in various places in the Aleutian Islands, and that these should represent ancestral Aleuts, there is as yet no unmistakable evidence to support this theory. Going back still earlier, some students of the region hold that the collection from the blade site on Anangula Island indicates the presence of these ancestral Aleuts at about 6000 bc, while other investigators maintain that there is no convincing evidence of occupational or ethnic continuity between the time represented by these materials and the earliest of the well-attested Aleut deposits of 3000 bc and after.

Shifting much later in time, research has plainly shown a recent period of rapid but narrowly restricted change in material culture, marked by the introduction of polished-slate ulus and certain other implement styles in what appears to have been a wave of influence sweeping the chain from the Alaska Peninsula to the Near Islands. Evidence from all but the easternmost zone suggests that this occurred after about A D 1500; some scholars place it even after the arrival of the Russian fur traders in the mid-eighteenth century, and credit the Russian practice of relocating the native fur hunters with the increase in communication and acculturation that is indicated by the changing styles of artifacts. In the eastern zone, evidence from the tip of the Alaska Peninsula and from Akun Island indicates that slate polishing had already gained a foothold at the end of the first millennium A D. Even here, however, despite the nearness of Eskimo territory, this late cultural intrusion did not overthrow local tradition.

When considered with Eskaleutian-speaking people as a whole, the Aleuts stand apart, diverging in speech and aspects of material culture and perhaps physique even from their cousins and near neighbours the Pacific Eskimos; and while they shared with these neighbours other aspects of material culture and of society, forming with them the western warm-water fringe of a single great northern people, they were yet protected from too much mainland influence by the watery distances of their long island chain.

In later times, when the Aleuts were subjected to the external pressures already referred to – pressures, as will be shown, reflecting a northern Eskimo expansion that would nearly overwhelm the people of the Kodiak region – the foreign wave seems to have spent itself in achieving a bare access to the mouth of the funnel formed by the Aleutian Islands. The Aleuts themselves, comfortably adapted to their surrounding seas, appear never to have turned back towards the mainland to send forth influences of their own. Isolated self-sufficiency seems always to have characterized their history.

CHAPTER V

People of the Later Tundra

All the archaeological traditions that remain to be discussed pertain to a zone which runs along the coastline stretching from Bristol Bay and the Alaska Peninsula on the south, northwards around Alaska, and eastwards across the top of the North American continent through the Arctic Archipelago to Greenland. This coastline, unlike those of Kodiak or the Aleutian Islands, is ice-bound in winter, and the terrain just inland is with few exceptions free of all vegetation taller than the people who occupied it.

Within this strip of herbaceous tundra and along its winter-frozen coastline, a zone ranging from only a few to several hundred kilometres broad, developed the ancestors of people now recognized as Eskimos. But during the several millennia of that development, there were some significant changes in the use that was made of the territory and its resources. The first of these adaptations is the subject of this chapter.

THE ARCTIC SMALL TOOL TRADITION

First discovered at Cape Denbigh on Norton Bay in Alaska, the *47* miniature implements of the far-flung Arctic Small Tool tradition are now known to occur throughout the area delineated above, from the Bering Sea side of the Alaska Peninsula to the narrow coastal strip of Greenland. Variety in stone tools is relatively restricted in the collections, which include small endblades and sideblades, often bipointed, and apparently designed to be inserted in the ends or sides of shafts or arrow- and spearheads made of hard organic material such as antler; burins struck on small bifaces; microblades; several kinds of carefully made scrapers; and occasional large knife-like bifaces. Other stone artifacts possibly present from the first appearance of the tradition include small adze blades with polished bits, and burin-like implements in which the usual percussion-formed burin facet is replaced by a polished face. Alaskan finds include no organic artifacts, for reasons of poor preservation in all the sites explored, and no oil lamps, but in the eastern Arctic bone needles, bone or antler foreshafts for arrows, and small bone harpoon heads are attributed to this period, while small elliptical stone lamps appeared before its end.

These two major zones of development of people of the Arctic Small Tool tradition will be treated separately.

47 Locations mentioned in regard to the Arctic Small Tool and Dorset traditions. In Alaska, sites of the Arctic Small Tool tradition occur north of the Alaska Peninsula within a strip of land adjacent to the coast, and are especially plentiful on the north slope of the Brooks Range. In Canada, sites of the same tradition occur throughout the Arctic Archipelago, in the Barren Grounds, on both sides of Hudson Bay, along

Alaska

The first finds were those called the Denbigh Flint complex, recovered from above Iyatayet Creek at Cape Denbigh on Norton Sound. The Denbigh Flint implements were stratified beneath those of two later cultures.

The Iyatayet Denbigh assemblage consists primarily of very numerous microblades and of a class of small burins; of the spalls removed as the burin tip was manufactured, some of them being used as tiny tips for engraving tools; of a series of well-formed endscrapers as well as other scraper-like implements called 'flake knives'; of a few triangular implement tips identified as harpoon endblades; and of a few larger knife blades. One especially notable class of implements is that of the plentiful

small sideblades and endblades, chipped bifacially and generally pointed at both ends, some of which are remarkable for the very delicate parallel flaking by which they were formed. At least one small adze blade, with a polished bit, first thought to have been mixed into the Denbigh Flint deposit from one of the overlying deposits, may now, on the basis of comparisons with other sites, in fact be said to belong to the Denbigh Flint complex.

Finds from other areas in Alaska have not always come up to the technological level apparent in the stone-working of the Denbigh Flint complex, nor have they all duplicated precisely the proportions of the various implements represented in that complex, but nevertheless they betray unmistakable resemblances to it. In the southernmost remains, for the northern Labrador coast, and in eastern, western and northern Greenland. Sites of the ensuing Dorset tradition are most plentiful around Foxe Basin, but with the exception of the Barren Grounds they occur at least sporadically in much of the eastern Arctic zone just mentioned, as well as in insular Newfoundland; they are not known as far west as the Mackenzie River.

instance – those from the Bering Sea slope of the Alaska Peninsula – both microblades and burins are greatly reduced in number and, though present, are rare. In one of the largest collections from Alaska, from the Brooks River locality in the Naknek River drainage, there are numerous examples of endblades of a delicacy of workmanship which rivals that exhibited in the Denbigh Flint complex, but there are also cruder artifacts without the fine ripple-flaking usually thought characteristic of the collection, and which in some cases have been recovered from the same living floors as the fine examples.

The site at Iyatayet showed no sign of the construction of permanent aboriginal dwellings, although the positions of fires were suggested by reddish discolourations and by fire-cracked pebbles, the latter being extremely common in most sites of the Arctic Small Tool tradition. It was concluded that the cultural debris at Iyatayet had been deposited directly on top of the surface sod in a temporary camp site. Although the only identifiable bone was a few fragments of charred seal bone, the nature of the tool assemblage, with its heavy preponderance of small sideblades and endblades for lances and arrows over the triangular blades thought to have been used with harpoons, led its excavator to conclude

48

48   Arctic Small Tool tradition, south-western Alaska: stone artifacts from the upper Naknek drainage system: *a*, microblade; *b*, burin; *c–e*, chalcedony projectile points; *f*, sideblade; *g*, scraper; *h*, adze blade with polished bit.

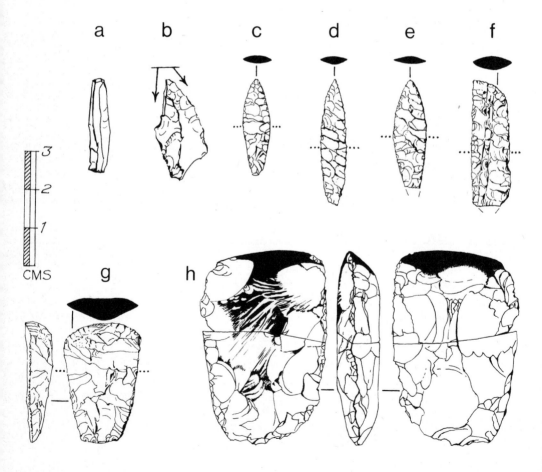

that the Denbigh camps were chiefly for the hunting of caribou rather than seal.

Elsewhere in Alaska, in the numerous sites that have been reported since the discovery of the Denbigh Flint complex, remains are also generally those of temporary camps. These may be located along the coast or farther inland in the tundra zone, especially along the course of streams. Remains of small fires are sometimes surrounded by a restricted zone in which artifacts and chips are scattered, perhaps marking the location of a small tent.

Constructed houses, apparently intended for winter occupation, are known thus far from only four locations, all of them between 50 and 250 kilometres from the coast: at Onion Portage on the Kobuk River; at Howard Pass between the Noatak and Colville drainages in the Brooks Range; and along the upper portions of both the Naknek and the Ugashik River systems on the Alaska Peninsula. At Brooks River, in the upper Naknek drainage, the remains are particularly numerous, and *49, 50* a total of fourteen houses have been tested extensively. Uniformly squarish and about 4 metres on the side, these had been excavated into the contemporary surface a depth varying from the thickness of the sod to as much as 50 centimetres, to be entered by an entryway that sloped into one side of the house like a tunnel. With a central fire that was sometimes surrounded by stones, the houses might also contain a box-like structure of vertical stone slabs, some 40 centimetres square, partially filled with yellow clay and flanked by a pile of fire-cracked stones apparently used with the box in some system of stone-boiling. Although the construction of the roofs is not understood precisely, the presence in the collapsed fill of the houses of numerous deposits of a distinctive yellow volcanic ash that was immediately below the sod at the time the houses were constructed, implies that at least parts of the roofs had been covered by sod chunks. In one case what seemed to be the moulds of four central posts were present around the fireplace area, but none was discovered in other excavations.

At least one similar square house appears to have been found at Howard Pass, far to the north, as well as in the earliest Arctic Small Tool component – the so-called Proto-Denbigh – from the site at Onion Portage on the Kobuk River. In this last site the somewhat later houses – of what is called Classic Denbigh – were round, excavated through the sod, and with a large stone-lined central hearth. These have been interpreted as being similar to certain temporary structures used by recent natives of the region: a framework of willow poles covered either with moss or with tents of a double thickness of caribou hide with hair in the centre, and which in extremely cold weather may be piled over with a layer of snow.

At Onion Portage and elsewhere in the interior, a primary aim of Small Tool people appears to have been the taking of caribou. Whereas this is also true on the Alaska Peninsula, the location there of camps and houses along streams that now receive substantial runs of migrating salmon suggests that summer fishing, too, was a focus of attention. Although there is no specific artifactual evidence which points to

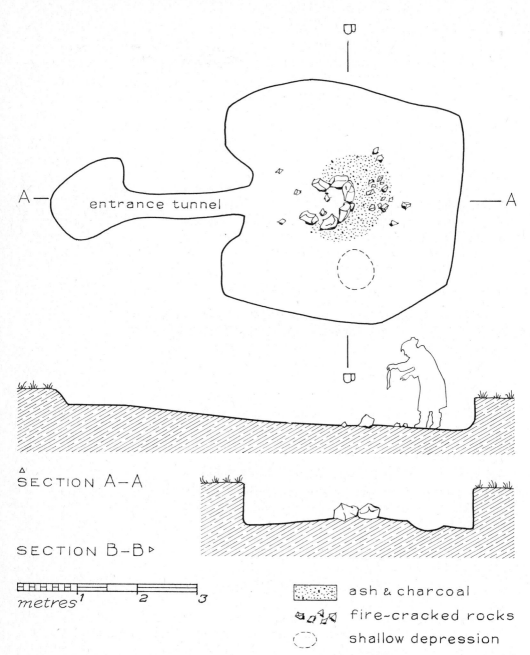

A —   — A

entrance tunnel

SECTION A–A

SECTION B–B ▷

metres   1   2   3

ash & charcoal
fire-cracked rocks
shallow depression

49   Arctic Small Tool tradition, south-western Alaska: plan and sections of a house in the upper Naknek River drainage; two nearby houses are radiocarbon dated to about 1450 and 1200 bc. The roof was apparently covered with sod.

fishing, fragmentary teeth of spawning-stage salmon and a few charred bones of trout have been recovered from floor debris. Coastal camp-sites, on the other hand, seem to have been for the seasonal hunting of seals, as is suggested by a certain amount of bone waste, despite the interpretation of the nature of the original coastal Denbigh Flint tool assemblage as the kit of caribou hunters.

Wherever cultural deposits of the Arctic Small Tool tradition occur in Alaska they seem to constitute a break in the continuity of occupation

50 Arctic Small Tool tradition, south-western Alaska: remains of a semi-subterranean house at Brooks River, upper Naknek drainage, radiocarbon dated to about 1450 bc. A pile of fire-cracked pebbles lies beside the central hearth. Four holes mark the location of stains that seem to be the remains of structural posts around the fireplace, but the find of post remnants has not been duplicated in any other such house (such as the similar one shown in Ill. 49). The light-coloured earth lying beneath the north arrow on the other side of the house, and which surrounds the aboriginal house excavation, is a layer of yellow volcanic ash that was immediately beneath the sod at the time the house was constructed. Spruce trees have invaded the region within the past 500 years; at the time the house was occupied the vegetation was chiefly grass with some alder, birch, and willow.

at a site. Where predecessors are known, they were people of the Northern Archaic tradition, who, after the irruption of the Small Tool peoples along the coastline, apparently withdrew to thrive in the forested regions farther inland. One partial exception to this rule was on the northern side of the Alaska Peninsula where people of Small Tool tradition appear to have replaced Northern Archaic people and also a second people of the Pacific coast (of the early Takli Birch phase, mentioned earlier), both of whom had it seems been making desultory use of the Bering Sea side of the Peninsula on a seasonal basis, probably for caribou hunting. For a millennium after this replacement, people of the Small Tool tradition and people of the Takli Birch phase of the Kodiak tradition continued to live on opposite slopes of the Peninsula, virtually without contact.

From consideration of geological and other evidence at Iyatayet, the final report on the original Denbigh Flint complex concluded that the assemblage dated from between 3000 and 2500 bc. Remains of Arctic Small Tool assemblages from elsewhere in Alaska, however, are generally dated by radiocarbon to the centuries following 2000 bc, and it now seems likely, given some inconsistencies in the Cape Denbigh evidence, that the Iyatayet deposit is of the same age. A single earlier assemblage is apparently that of the Proto-Denbigh of Onion Portage, where endblades and scrapers, cruder than those of the Denbigh Flint complex at Iyatayet, seem to be securely dated to about 2200 bc.

The Eastern Arctic

There is general agreement among archaeologists that the appearance of the Arctic Small Tool tradition in Canada and Greenland – the first known occupation by man in most of the region – was the result of a migratory movement from the west. Unfortunately, the details of this migration are not at all clear. Indeed, given the variation in material culture that is manifested by apparently contemporaneous sites in the zone, when compared either among themselves or with Small Tool collections from Alaska, two things seem certain: the very earliest of these migrants are known only patchily, if at all; and a number of changes in the forms of tools must have begun to occur immediately upon their makers' expansion into the new zone.

The archaeological remains of the east are presently divisible into two consecutive stages within the Arctic Small Tool tradition. The first of these can be designated the Independence stage. Named after Independence Fjord in extreme north-eastern Greenland, the collections included seem to represent the earliest known bearers of the Arctic Small Tool tradition in the east, dating from 2000 bc to 1700 bc. Interestingly enough, these collections are from the extreme north, sites of this stage having been found with certainty only in the area between Devon Island in the Arctic Archipelago, and thence north- and eastward to Peary Land in northern Greenland – the northernmost landmass in the world, all of it at least 1,200 kilometres north of Point Barrow, Alaska – where some of the sites are no more than 700 kilometres from the North Pole.

51 Arctic Small Tool tradition, eastern Arctic, Independence stage: stone projectile tips and ivory harpoon head from Port Refuge, Devon Island; length of the harpoon head, about 6.2 cm. The small harpoon head, which is not designed to toggle, is slotted at the tip to receive a small triangular endblade, probably of stone.

Although the portable artifacts of the Independence collections are obviously similar to Alaskan materials, there are some noticeable differences. As in Alaska, common implements are small burins, microblades, triangular endscrapers and symmetrical endblades apparently made for insertion into a hard foreshaft, while there are no stone lamps. But, unlike most Alaskan collections, a high proportion of the Independence endblades contain a clearly set off and tapering stem; there   51 is more serration of implement edges; evidence for polished burins and adzes is lacking; and most implements are slightly larger.

Again unlike Alaska, where bone or antler artifacts of the Arctic Small Tool tradition have almost never survived, in the Independence sites a number of organic implements have been recovered. These include bone needles, indicative of the use of sewn and presumably tailored clothing; fragments of bone arrowheads; and two harpoon heads, from the locale on Devon Island, which have a drilled hole for the line, and were designed to hold victims by barbs, rather than by toggling (twisting crosswise in the wound). In the Greenland sites an absence of harpoon heads is not surprising, since virtually all bone waste in these sites is of musk ox, suggesting that sea-mammal hunting was not an important pastime of the earliest Greenlanders.

The Greenland settlements have been interpreted as both summer and winter sites, distinguishable by the presence of adjacent food-cache pits at the winter habitations, and flagstone forecourts in front of the summer houses, where many activities could take place during the sunny days and nights. The dwellings themselves survive chiefly as so-called 'mid-   52 passages' of flagstones, often bisecting the area formed by an elliptical ring of stones. Such mid-passages consist of a pair of parallel lines of

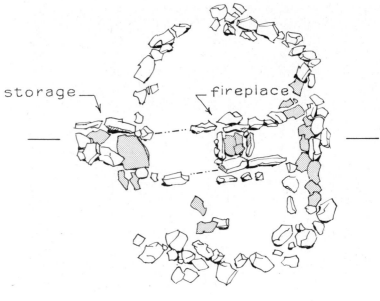

storage

fireplace

metres ¹ 2 3

paving stones

52 Arctic Small Tool tradition, eastern Arctic, Independence stage: plan of a dwelling – probably a tent – from Independence Fjord in northern Greenland, radiocarbon dated to about 1700 bc. A portion of the central 'passage' appears to have been removed, possibly to build the small storage structure just outside the encircling stones.

vertically set flagstones, 50 centimetres or slightly more apart, with a separate square hearth of similar vertical flagstones set off towards the centre of this demarcated area.

That these habitation ruins indicate the original presence of tents is suggested by the fact that there are no soil deposits of the kind that would be expected to result from the erosion of sod walls, nor was there any significant excavation into the subsoil. Further, the use of interior fires of animal bones, local willow twigs, or driftwood (which is brought to north-eastern Greenland by ocean and ice currents from Siberia) argues against the use of snow alone for houses, in the manner known from later Canadian Eskimos, since the amount of heat generated by an open fire – unlike the small flame of an oil lamp – would melt the inside of a snow-house to an intolerable extent.

To judge from the debris, the 'passage' itself apparently served as a kitchen and food-preparation zone. The placing of the flagstones along the passage, as well as the distribution of artifacts (concentrated by those vertical flagstones), suggest that the areas on each side of the food-preparation zone were covered with musk-ox hides, which, with the use of similar hides for the roof, doubled and with the hair inside and covered with snow when necessary, would have made fairly snug quarters in which to while away the two-and-a-half months of total darkness of the north Greenland winter.

While the Independence people of Greenland concentrated on musk oxen and a few other large land mammals, those on north-western Devon Island gathered to hunt the abundant local sea mammals. At Port Refuge off the south coast of Grinnell Peninsula, in a region kept largely free of ice by wind and ocean currents, they left behind traces of the same sorts of dwellings and artifacts as the Greenland folk, plus two non-toggling harpoon heads, one of ivory, the other of antler, as well as plentiful bones of seal and much rarer bones of caribou, musk ox, and waterfowl.

The second stage of the Arctic Small Tool tradition in the east is known as Pre-Dorset. The majority of finds pertaining to the tradition within the eastern Arctic are placed here, in a somewhat heterogeneous manifestation that must begin by 1700 bc and ends at a somewhat arbitrarily assigned date of about 800 bc, when the succeeding Dorset tradition may be declared fully developed.

Presumably, the Pre-Dorset is an outgrowth of the earlier Independence stage, although the presence of Independence peoples in the major zones of Pre-Dorset occupation – that is, in the eastern Canadian Arctic north of Hudson Bay and in western Greenland – is implied rather than proved by the evidence, and some archaeologists prefer to view each stage as the result of a separate migration from the Alaskan homeland. Indeed, the only area in which Pre-Dorset follows Independence fairly clearly is at Port Refuge, mentioned above, where a brief foray by Pre-Dorset people north of the main Pre-Dorset region apparently postdated the Independence presence there. To some extent, then, Independence and Pre-Dorset 'stages' may be regional variants, although convincing arguments can be presented for the temporal priority of at least the earliest Independence folk over those of Pre-Dorset.

Pre-Dorset may itself be divided into at least two major regional variants, one centred on a core zone in north-eastern Canada immediately north of Hudson Bay, including the shores of Hudson Strait and the land surrounding the Foxe Basin, and a second centred on western Greenland, well south of the region of the earlier Independence occupation. This Greenland variety of Pre-Dorset is termed Sarqaq.

In Canadian regions outside the core zone, occupation by Arctic Small Tool tradition people is interrupted by certain discontinuities through time. The early inhabitants of northern Labrador, present by 1700 bc or even before, vanished around 1500 bc. And despite the fact that Pre-Dorset progenitors are presumed to have traversed the area during their original migration from Alaska, Pre-Dorset sites east of the Mackenzie River and in the southern Arctic Archipelago are to be found in significant numbers only after about 1500 bc, when the nature of the finds suggests that the immediate source of these western Pre-Dorset people lay in the core region of Pre-Dorset development north of

Hudson Bay. East of Hudson Bay, there is a Pre-Dorset presence at about this same time, and then or a little later – by 1200 bc – there began a further west- and southward expansion of Pre-Dorset people on to the Barren Grounds, where they reached as far south as what is now northern Manitoba, and at least as far south-west as Great Slave Lake. This last movement appears to have been related to the range of the major Barren Grounds caribou herds, illustrating the continuing interest in the pursuit of herds of land mammals. All these outlying Pre-Dorset people, on the central Canadian coast, on the Barrens and east of Hudson Bay, apparently disappeared at about the end of the Pre-Dorset period, as the territory of occupation once again contracted to the heartland around the Foxe Basin and Hudson Strait.

With the Pre-Dorset occupation of north-eastern Canada there are definite divergences from artifacts of the Independence stage, in some cases away from the forms of implements known from the Arctic Small Tool tradition in Alaska, and in some cases closer to those forms. Like many Alaskan collections, the Canadian assemblages possess small burins, the flat faces of which have been polished, as well as occasional polished burin-like tools in which a polished facet replaces the scar of the usual burin-blow, and polished adze blades. The assemblages also include some double-tapered or bipointed endblades for insertion into a hard arrow foreshaft. But unlike the Alaskan assemblages, the Pre-Dorset collections may have knives of chipped stone with notches on the sides to facilitate hafting, occasional knives or other such cutting implements of polished slate, and now and then a rare elliptical stone lamp. Completely absent is the fine degree of workmanship exhibited by the best ripple-flaked projectile blades of the Denbigh Flint complex.

Although many of the sites yielded no perishable artifacts, some produced the earliest toggling harpoon heads of the area, with sockets open on one side so that the foreshaft must be lashed in, and without stone endblades; numerous needles; and long, open-socketed lance heads, some of them with slots or open seats at the point to receive a separate stone blade. Bow-and-arrow fragments are clearly identifiable. Bone waste includes that of musk ox, caribou, polar bear, and birds. But implements of ivory and of seal and walrus bone, as well as the presence of the harpoon heads, indicate the importance of sea mammals, a focus also suggested by the coastal location of the majority of sites.

Habitation remains are consistently of what is regarded in the Eskimo-Aleut region as temporary construction. Summer sites may be indicated by tent rings – elliptical lines of stones enclosing areas some 2 metres long and $1\frac{1}{2}$ metres wide – or at times simply by elliptical zones yielding artifacts and small rocks, in which bone waste and artifacts are mixed into the surface soil. Winter occupations may be indicated by similar zones of artifacts in which a few small rocks covered with the soot of burned fat attest the use of diminutive oil fires, and in which tools are confined to the upper ground surface with no bone refuse present – presumably because the bone was deposited in snow, to be laid cleanly upon the surface with the spring thaw, when it was dispersed by birds and animals. These artifact zones are interpreted as the sites of snow-block shelters covered with portable roofs of skins, or of complete dome-shaped snow houses such as those used by recent Central Eskimos. Where the so-called mid-passage is found, it has been thought to indicate an earlier presence of Independence people, although in at least one case, at the Seahorse Gully site, near Churchill, Manitoba, a mid-passage was reported in a square stone alignment that yielded Pre-Dorset, rather than Independence, implements.

During the centuries after 1700 bc in which the eastern Canadian Pre-Dorset persisted, characteristic tools such as side-notched knives, polished burins, polished burin-like implements, and polished slate knives tended to increase in frequency, while in some areas the miniaturization of tools already so evident in the Arctic Small Tool tradition was carried to still greater extremes. In Greenland, on the other hand, the Sarqaq collections of the same date seem to retain a much greater affinity with contemporary Alaskan assemblages, thereby exhibiting what has been referred to as an archaic Arctic Small Tool cast, although some of the Sarqaq tools tend to exceed the comparable Alaskan specimens in size. A similar archaic cast seems evident in some collections from northern Labrador.

53

The Beginning and the Ending

Bearers of the Arctic Small Tool tradition were present in Alaska at least as early as 2200 bc, and had spread east to northern Greenland by 2000 bc. The absence of significant numbers of permanent habitations in northern Alaska and the eastern Arctic makes it clear that these people were nomadic, while the distribution of their sites and the nature of their

53 Arctic Small Tool tradition, Greenland Pre-Dorset (Sarqaq): left to right: two stone projectile blades, two burins, adze blade with polished bit, and scraper (below); length of item on the left, 7.3 cm. As is usual with Sarqaq burins, the faces at the upper end of the two pieces – but not the burin facets themselves – are polished.

bone waste and artifact assemblages suggest strongly that they were specially adapted to the pursuit of land mammals on the tundra, although they also visited the coast to hunt seals. Despite their nomadism, there is no direct evidence to prove that they used boats, and the presence of dogs – the draft animals of later Eskimos – is attested in only a very few sites. Nevertheless, it is difficult to conceive of their moving through the vast territory of the Arctic without some form of transport other than the human back.

One speculation is that the Arctic Small Tool people made their way eastwards originally by relying upon the hunting of the musk ox, an animal that by its habit of forming stationary, compact herds when threatened, is particularly easy to slaughter. If this was the case, it is conceivable that the migration to the east might have been hastened by a tendency to butcher the musk oxen so rapidly that hunting territories were quickly depleted. Outside Greenland, however, the evidence does not seem to indicate that there was any such preference for a single prey, despite the presence of the musk ox throughout the Arctic at one time.

In any event, once established in the Canadian Arctic the Arctic Small Tool people concentrated on caribou, and engaged in at least a seasonal hunting of seals. We have no proof at this time, however, of the use of specialized techniques for winter sealing through the ice.

Because the earliest of these people known in Alaska appear to represent a break in the local occupational sequence, their origin is the subject of some debate. Some archaeologists have maintained that their roots must lie within Alaska, in the much earlier Palaeo-arctic tradition. Others argue that virtually all their distinctive tools were at least prototypically present by the third millennium bc in the Siberian Neolithic, and that the appearance of Arctic Small Tool people in Alaska is the simple result of a migration from Siberia at this time. More specifically, the Neolithic Bel'kachinsk culture of the Aldan River region, dated to the third millennium, includes very small and finely chipped bifaces, scrapers and burins which are highly reminiscent of implements of the Arctic Small Tool tradition, so that despite the presence of pottery in the Aldan assemblages the Bel'kachinsk culture would seem to be a distant counterpart of the American tradition. Similar and non-ceramic correspondences are provided by the early Neolithic of the Kamchatka Peninsula and collections known from sites in the vicinity of the Anadyr River. This Asian evidence appears to imply that in the tundra regions of eastern Siberia there developed the major elements that coalesced sometime before 2000 bc into the Arctic Small Tool tradition as it is known in America. Thus while the origins of the Small Tool tradition undoubtedly lie in the Palaeo-arctic tradition, its evolution need not necessarily have taken place east of Bering Strait.

The demise of the Arctic Small Tool tradition is also something of a mystery. In the region of major occupation in the eastern Arctic, the Pre-Dorset developed smoothly into the Dorset tradition, to be discussed shortly. In the west, however, there is less certainty. At about the time that the Pre-Dorset hunters vanished from the Barren Grounds of Canada, Arctic Small Tool people also disappeared from the major region of occupation in the upper Naknek drainage on the Alaska Peninsula. By now, if not some centuries earlier, they had also vanished from the Brooks Range to the north. Indeed, in every region of Alaska in which they are found, their disappearance is followed by at least a short hiatus, before new cultural developments appear. So dramatic is this hiatus, despite the fact that the specific time of its occurrence may not be exactly contemporaneous in both northern and southern Alaska, that it seems as if the major resource base of the Small Tool peoples had been suddenly removed. Unfortunately, no firm evidence is available. But, as is usual when discussing the prehistory of Arctic regions, it is possible to speculate about the effects of changes in climate.

The post-glacial Thermal Maximum gave way to a stable cooling trend which lasted from about 3000 to 1500 bc. This period would have seen the initial movements of Small Tool people to the east, and the Independence stage occupation of the High Arctic. Sometime around 1500 bc, however, a significantly colder and less stable interval began which lasted until 1200 or 1100 bc. As far north as Peary Land the already marginal climate may simply have become unbearable, for this cold interval seems to coincide with the withdrawal from the High Arctic. It was apparently the same cold interval, paradoxically, which witnessed the expansion of Pre-Dorset people from the Hudson Bay heartland westwards along the central Canadian coast and into the Barren Grounds, and saw important Small Tool incursions in the Brooks Range and on the Alaska Peninsula. A key to understanding this more southerly expansion of Arctic Small Tool people may be the effect of increased cold on caribou territories, since colder climate decreases the likelihood of alternate thawing and freezing in mid-winter, preserving the powdery snow through which the northern caribou feed most efficiently, and so perhaps inducing an expansion in their winter range. Following this cold interval, the climate warmed again, and the Small Tool people disappeared from their southern territories, possibly this time because of a climatically stimulated contraction in the range of caribou.

On the other hand, one must be wary of any facile climatic explanation, since relatively localized fluctuations in air currents may be more important to local climates than are continental trends, and in particular since the specific responses to climatic changes by human beings, even nomadic hunters, depend upon social and intellectual conditions quite beyond the change in climate itself.

THE DORSET TRADITION

In a number of areas in the eastern Arctic – indeed, in all those outside the central zone of Pre-Dorset occupation north of Hudson Bay – there is a period apparently of abandonment around or not long after 1000 bc.

94

When sites of the Dorset tradition do make their appearance in these regions, there is a marked difference between the material culture they yield and that of the earlier Pre-Dorset.

To generalize, the Dorset stone artifacts are characterized by an emphasis on side-notching of endblades, the introduction of slate knives and polished burin-like tools, the consistent use of stone lamps and the appearance of a technique for sharpening endblades by pushing off a long flute-like flake from the tip. These introductions tend to coincide with the abandonment of chipped burins, of stemmed endblades and of certain kinds of scrapers. Changes such as these led some early investigators to propose that Dorset culture was in significant measure derived from new immigrants, possibly people from the south.

In certain regions within the area of major Dorset development, however, discontinuity is not indicated, and the distinction between Pre-Dorset and Dorset becomes blurred. Southern Baffinland is the most fully reported of these regions. Here most of the characteristic Dorset stone artifacts were present before the end of the second millennium bc, and although after about 800 bc there was an increase in the proportions of these – polished burin-like tools, side-notched implements, polished slate – there was no sharp break in development. It is true that some innovations occurred early in the Dorset period: nephrite was first used as a material for polished implements – burin-like tools and adze blades; the small stone lamp appeared throughout the area, sometimes rectangular in shape now, and with it a small cup-sized pot of soapstone, grooved for suspension over the lamp and presumably used for cooking. But the degree of continuity with Pre-Dorset in the forms of the great majority of material objects is so unmistakable that the only conclusion now justifiable is that the Dorset people were descended almost wholly from their Pre-Dorset predecessors.

Throughout the eastern Arctic, the preservation of organic materials is consistently better from Dorset times than from previous periods, so that characteristic Dorset artifacts in these materials are familiar. Unfortunately, the paucity of Pre-Dorset organic tools prevents a systematic study being made of the kinds of changes that occurred in these artifacts. Indeed, only in the Igloolik region are there enough organic implements known from Pre-Dorset times for some idea of these changes to be gained. Here, small bone sled shoes are apparently clearly new, as are broad bone knives interpreted as snow-knives, similar to those used by later Eskimos to cut blocks of snow for the construction of their dome-shaped snow-houses. Other new introductions are spiked ivory or antler devices known as ice-creepers, designed to be strapped to the soles of the feet when walking over ice, and used in later times especially for seal-hunting. A lance with a bifurcated socket is present throughout the Dorset period, and ivory and bone needles, together with some fragments of skin garments, indicate the continued practice of tailoring. A few parts and models of what are thought to be small kayaks are reported. Above all, Dorset harpoon heads are plentiful, appearing early in the Dorset period with a substantially closed socket, although

54 Dorset tradition: left to right: chipped-stone side-notched knife, two projectile blades and two polished-stone projectile or knife blades from various sites in Canada; length of knife, 4.8 cm.

55 Dorset tradition: left to right: two chipped-stone points and three polished-stone projectile or knife blades from sites in western Greenland.

56 Dorset tradition: polished-stone burin-like objects from western Greenland; length of the longest, 4.3 cm. Functionally, implements such as these appear to have replaced the earlier burin with a struck burin-facet.

61

57

58–60

variously formed, and returning to an open socket in the later Dorset. But despite evidence for some increase in the efficiency of transport and hunting, other changes seem retrogressive and inexplicable: the bow and arrow, for example, fell out of use at this time, while dogs were scarcely present at all.

In addition to the existence of snow-knives, evidence for the continued use of temporary dwellings of snow is provided by the same kinds of clearly circumscribed surface deposits of artifacts mentioned for the Pre-Dorset. The regular use of the small stone lamp offered a means not widespread earlier of lighting and moderately heating the snow-house. Tent rings – circular or rectangular alignments of stones – continue, and may enclose a line of upright stone slabs in a manner reminiscent of the mid-passage of Independence habitations.

In addition to the more ephemeral dwellings, there are in some places soily midden accumulations which are heavy enough to suggest that sods were used for house or shelter walls. And in a number of locations there are what can be interpreted as relatively permanent winter houses, some $2\frac{1}{2}$ by 5 metres in size, with a central floor dug 40–50 centimetres into the ground, having sleeping benches on two or three sides along the walls, and a central fireplace. In Baffinland one such house yielded sticks of driftwood from a roof skeleton of a sort which suggested that a skin covering had been used; this might have been heaped over with a layer of snow.

Taking these indications together, one can conclude that in Dorset times there was at least some increase in sedentism, although it is likely that the majority of habitations were still temporary or portable. Furthermore, in middens the proportion of sea-mammal remains, especially seal, now often exceeded the proportion of bones of caribou, clearly suggesting an increase in the use of sea resources. A shift towards the coast seems to be indicated also by the virtual absence of inland sites of the Dorset tradition. Although this last circumstance may be the result of incomplete knowledge, it is probably significant that sites of the Pre-Dorset have frequently been reported in the interior, despite the fact that the Pre-Dorset period is no more than a millennium in length and the period in which the Dorset tradition flourished is nearly twice as long. There is still no evidence in Dorset sites, however, of the specialized equipment used by later peoples of the Arctic coast for hunting seals through the winter ice at their breathing-holes.

Although we have no proof of a Dorset expansion into the Barren Grounds similar to that of their predecessors, remains have been found of an early Dorset occupation of the High Arctic which took place in the first half of the first millennium bc, involving the same inhospitable area as that of the earlier Independence stage of the Arctic Small Tool tradition – roughly that from Devon Island to north-eastern Greenland. Around the beginning of the Christian era this High Arctic occupation disappeared, but Dorset folk are also found in western Greenland, where their culture may be presumed to have derived in large part from the preceding and local Sarqaq culture, although some archaeologists have

57–61 Dorset tradition: artifacts from sites in northern Canada: (far left: two views) cloven-footed lance – the stepped bed at the tip (above) would have held an end-blade, and the pair of grooves in the side (near the bottom) two sideblades (length, 20 cm); (top right: three views) harpoon head – the face of a seal is lightly suggested at the blade slot on the tip (length, 8 cm); (middle row) two harpoon heads, the longer one (length, 7.5 cm) with a chipped-stone endblade inserted, the other (length, 3.5 cm) in two views; (below) ice-creeper of antler made to be lashed to the feet (length, 12.5 cm).

been more inclined to conceive of the Dorset presence as the result of a new, important migration from the west.

These are not the only indications of Dorset expansion. By 500 bc Dorset people were present on the central Canadian coast, and had moved south along the west coast of Hudson Bay to present-day Manitoba; at the same time they also moved south along the coasts of northern and central Labrador, from where by the beginning of the Christian era they were apparently dislodged by Indians of the interior who pushed to the coast. These latter Dorset folk, however, were able to expand farther southwards and establish a presence in insular Newfoundland which endured for several centuries.

To summarize, there was a clear continuity of occupation from the Pre-Dorset to the Dorset periods north of Hudson Bay, and probably also in western Greenland. The same may be true in parts of the central Canadian coast west of Hudson Bay, although investigators here have been more inclined to view the occupation as intermittent. In any event, from these areas the Dorset migrated into the High Arctic, south along the west coast of Hudson Bay and south to Labrador and Newfoundland. Such forays punctuated a period of 2000 years during which there was a stable adaptation to the Arctic environment, and within which fluctuations in implement styles occurred as relatively minor variations around the central Dorset theme.

As with the preceding Arctic Small Tool period, it is possible to speculate on the relationship between some broadly indicated climatic changes and the distribution of Dorset population. The period of occupation of the High Arctic by Dorset folk, around 700 bc, seems to have been one of relative warmth, the period of withdrawal one of increasing cold. This same interval of deteriorating climate – 500 bc and after – may well coincide with the expansion of Dorset folk to the west and south.

Again, however, it is probably unwise to press such apparent coincidences. What one can state unequivocally is that Dorset cultural stability was maintained throughout the eastern Arctic until the years around AD 1000, when the Dorset folk were overrun by people from Alaska – like themselves, ultimately descended from bearers of the Arctic Small Tool tradition – who brought a new way of life to the eastern Arctic. Dorset culture as it had been practised ceased to exist, but not before Dorset people had become the first of the properly American natives – the Skraelings of the early Norse sagas – to be encountered by Europeans in their expansion to Greenland and the New World.

Dorset Art
The survival of organic artifacts in relative plenty has permitted the recovery of some pieces – albeit few in proportion to the total number of artifacts – that can clearly be construed as art. With few exceptions – including most spectacularly a pair of wooden masks from northern Baffinland – these are miniature carvings executed in wood, ivory, antler, or occasionally bone.

In one study which considered a substantial number of the known objects of Dorset art, a total of 125 objects were found to provide 151 recognizable subjects of representation. A third of these subjects were human beings, a quarter sea mammals, a fifth bears, about 11 per cent *62, 64* birds, only 4 per cent caribou, and the remainder fish, weasels, and *63* others. Accepting the intrinsic interest of humans in themselves, the high proportion of sea mammals represented parallels the high proportion of Dorset midden bone waste that these creatures supply. The number of bears, however, seems to reflect an interest somewhat out of proportion to the place of the bear in mundane life, suggesting some ceremonial, supernatural, or at least imaginative interest in this morphologically man-like mammal of the north.

In one well-documented site three bear figures – two of them enclosed in a decorated bone case – were recovered from the immediate vicinity of a human mandible and three ribs, suggesting to the excavator that the art objects represented grave furniture for a body which had been formally disposed of at ground level. The circumstance also suggested to him that

62–64   Dorset tradition: (left) miniature wooden mask from Button Point, Bylot Island, northern Baffinland (length, 6 cm); (right) joined pair of ivory swans (lower, length 6 cm) and single ivory swan (length, 4.2 cm), all from Mansel Island, northern Hudson Bay; (below) ivory floating bear (length, 15.2 cm), Igloolik region.

the objects may have had a special significance as amulets or even as part of a shaman's ritual paraphernalia.

In possible support of this same line of reasoning, small wooden figures of game animals from a Dorset site at Button Point, on Bylot Island off the north coast of Baffinland, have a small cut between the shoulder blades into which a sliver of wood has been pushed; the same site yields similar carvings of humans with small slits in the chest. Altogether this evidence implies that at least some of the Dorset art objects may have had a magical function. On the other hand, the elaborated aspect of certain Dorset harpoon heads, into which animal forms are worked, suggests more in the nature of amused play on the part of the craftsmen.

Unfortunately, the traditional origins of Dorset art are obscure. That is to say, it is not possible to judge to what extent the style derives from some representational proclivity on the part of their forbears of the Arctic Small Tool tradition. One might argue that this gap in our knowledge is largely the result of the extreme inadequacy of the sample of organic artifacts from Small Tool sites, for it seems clear from the care that was taken with the best stone artifacts by some early Small Tool craftsmen that an aesthetic, as well as a functional, aim was pursued. On present evidence, however, elaboration of Small Tool organic implements seems confined to occasional rather simple and uninspired engraved lines.

CHAPTER VI

People of the Bering and Chukchi Seas

In the east cultural development was gradual, although the centuries immediately following 1000 bc witnessed changes in artifacts which were pronounced enough to give rise to the distinction between the Dorset and Arctic Small Tool traditions. In the west, on the other hand, the analogous transformation was more nearly revolutionary, causing a general cultural re-orientation which led directly to what two millennia later would be recognized as a characteristically Eskimo way of life. For as this western development achieved its promise, it expanded to encompass all the territory ever occupied by people of the Arctic Small Tool tradition, and more.

As was mentioned earlier, in both northern and southern Alaska the continuity of occupation seems to have been interrupted after the apparently sudden disappearance of the Arctic Small Tool tradition. In the north, at least, this disappearance was followed quite quickly by indications of the presence of various groups which appear to partake of Arctic Small Tool ancestry, and of others of alien origin.

At Cape Krusenstern, just north of Kotzebue Sound on the Chukchi Sea coast, a major archaeological study has focused upon a long sequence of cultures. These are located on a massive set of ocean-beach ridges which have been forming successively at the surf line ever since the sea reached its present level around 3000 bc. The beaches farthest inland – numbers 78 to 104, counting from the present shoreline – have revealed scattered camp-sites of Arctic Small Tool people. Immediately outside these, in a single restricted location on beach 53, were found occupation remains of what was termed the Old Whaling culture. Radiocarbon evidence suggests a date of about 1700 bc.

Five deep semi-subterranean houses were thought to have been for winter use, and five shallow houses for the summer. Refuse consisted chiefly of whalebone. Tools included chipped-stone lance-heads, knives, and chipped blades which are assumed to have been for large whaling harpoons. The tools are not obviously comparable to those known from anywhere else.

Although archaeologists always expect to find evidence for idiosyncratic acts by individuals or isolated historical incidents, they are still inclined to try to fit new discoveries into the framework of the main course of development of whatever culture or cultural sequence they may be studying. In this case, however, it appears beyond question that the small Old Whaling community on Cape Krusenstern, out of place both temporally and culturally, did indeed represent a temporary stay of a year

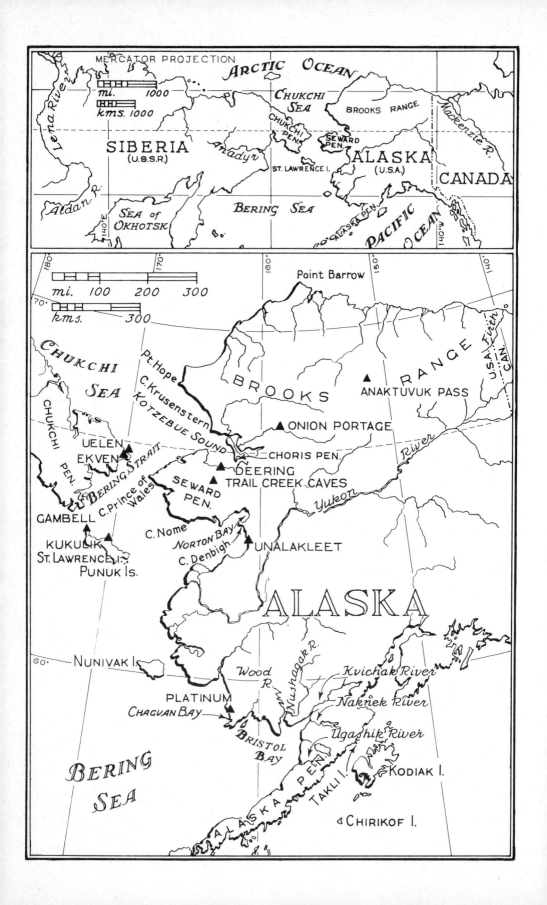

Top map:

MERCATOR PROJECTION

ARCTIC OCEAN

mi. 1000

kms. 1000

CHUKCHI SEA

BROOKS RANGE

Mackenzie R.

Lena River

CHUKCHI PEN.

SEWARD PEN.

SIBERIA (U.S.S.R.)

Anadyr

ALASKA (U.S.A.)

CANADA

ST. LAWRENCE I.

Aldan R.

Sea of OKHOTSK

BERING SEA

ALASKA PEN.

PACIFIC OCEAN

140°E

140°W

Bottom map:

180°

170°

160°

150°

140°

mi. 100 200 300

kms. 300

70°

Point Barrow

CHUKCHI SEA

Pt. Hope

C. Krusenstern

KOTZEBUE SOUND

BROOKS RANGE

ANAKTUVUK PASS

U.S.A. CAN.

ONION PORTAGE

UELEN

EKVEN

CHUKCHI PEN.

BERING STRAIT

CHORIS PEN.

DEERING

TRAIL CREEK CAVES

River

C. Prince of Wales

SEWARD PEN.

Yukon

GAMBELL

C. Nome

NORTON BAY

C. Denbigh

UNALAKLEET

KUKULIK

ST. LAWRENCE I.

PUNUK IS.

ALASKA

NUNIVAK I.

60°

Wood R.

Nushagak R.

Kvichak River

Naknek River

PLATINUM

CHAGVAN BAY

Ugashik River

BRISTOL BAY

ALASKA PEN.

KODIAK I.

TAKLI I.

CHIRIKOF I.

BERING SEA

or little more by some small group of coastal outlanders. Their house and artifact styles cannot easily be related to any well-documented archaeo-logical region, but common sense suggests that they were from somewhere around the North Pacific. Although the assemblage seems to represent the earliest example of a truly maritime economic orientation known in northern Eskimo territory, there is no evidence that these people, whoever they may have been, had any impact at all upon Alaskan cultural developments of the time. They are, however, a part of the diversity that becomes apparent with the disappearance of the Arctic Small Tool tradition.

65 Locations mentioned in relation to the Norton and early Thule traditions. Pure Norton tradition sites are so far known only in Alaska, although scattered evidence suggests they should also occur in easternmost Siberia. The slightly later sites of the Old Bering Sea stage of the Thule tradition are known only from the Chukchi Peninsula and islands about Bering Strait.

THE NORTON TRADITION

For present purposes the tradition of tool-making termed Norton will include all collections which have been referred by various scholars to the Norton culture – named after Norton Bay, where the first such collection was obtained – as well as those somewhat earlier collections assigned to Choris culture and the somewhat later ones known as Ipiutak culture. Of these, Norton and Choris assemblages are characterized by the presence of a variety of chipped-stone implements many of which are strongly reminiscent of those of the Arctic Small Tool tradition, of crudely scraped and polished slate (often rare), of oil lamps, and of the earliest kind of Alaskan pottery. Ipiutak assemblages lack oil lamps, polished slate, and pottery, but they are so similar to Norton collections in chipped-stone artifacts that recognition of them as a variant of the more widespread Norton tradition seems justified. The Norton tradition, as conceived here, therefore includes all post-Small Tool archaeological manifestations of Alaska usually termed Palaeo-Eskimo.

Choris Stage

The earliest known aspect of the Norton tradition occurs in the area north of Bering Strait, and is called Choris from the location of the first finds. The original collections, dating from shortly after 1000 bc, were from large elliptical houses (some of them 12 metres long) which had been excavated into the contemporary surface at a site on the Choris Peninsula at Kotzebue Sound. The pottery, in use for the first time in the Eskimo-Aleut region of North America, was made with inclusions of fibre such as hair or grass to reduce cracking during manufacture, and was decorated all over the exterior with linear stamping – narrow impressed corrugations that resulted from paddling the moist clay surface at random with a grooved stick. Compared with the earlier Arctic Small Tool tradition, the use of microblades has been abandoned, the use of burins has changed or been abandoned, projectile points are larger, adze blades are fully chipped rather than partially ground, and the oil lamp is in use. At the original Choris Peninsula site bone waste was predominantly that of caribou, despite the coastal location.

At Cape Krusenstern, most of the scanty finds thought to relate to this Choris stage derived from small camp-sites scattered along certain of the

66

67

beach ridges, and consist mainly of scraps of the characteristic pottery and of a few stone implements. Such bone waste as is represented is apparently from sea mammals. On a relatively early one of the same *68* beach ridges was found a spectacularly large cache of chipped lanceolate projectile or spear points, strikingly similar in many respects to some of the unfluted lanceolate points of certain early assemblages of the North American plains, including those termed Scottsbluff and Angostura. The cache probably also related to the Choris culture occupation.

Other collections of material which are clearly Choris are few. Lanceolate points similar to those of the Cape Krusenstern cache were found in the middle levels of the Trail Creek caves on the Seward Peninsula, which may date to the time of the Choris stage of the Norton tradition, but there were no other obvious Choris items in the rather mixed deposits. The undated Kayuk complex of Anaktuvuk Pass in the central Brooks Range also contains similar points and is thought by some to be related to the Choris stage, although others disagree. At Onion Portage on the Kobuk River the occupation of the corresponding period, although probably connected with Choris, is said to display some variation from the finds on the Choris Peninsula. The same appears to be

66 Plan and section of a Choris dwelling from Choris Peninsula, radiocarbon dated to about 700 bc. The dashed line indicates the limit of ground staining, possibly outside the dwelling itself. The nature of the roof is unknown.

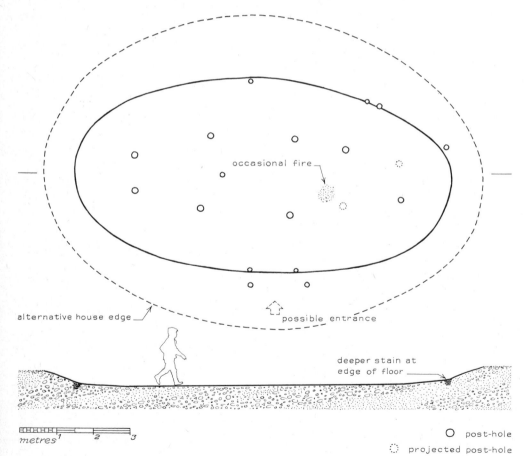

alternative house edge

possible entrance

occasional fire

deeper stain at edge of floor

metres

○ post-hole

⠂ projected post-hole

67 Norton tradition: potsherd of the early Norton tradition from the Iyatayet site, Cape Denbigh. The linear-stamped decoration is especially characteristic of the Choris stage of the tradition; height, 14 cm.

68 Norton tradition, Choris stage: three of a total cache of some 60 projectile points found on a Choris-period beach ridge at Cape Krusenstern; length of largest, 17.5 cm.

true at other locations. At one site immediately south of Barrow a complex including the characteristic Choris ceramics as well as small stone implements strongly reminiscent of those of the Arctic Small Tool tradition has been dated by radiocarbon to the late second millennium bc. An analogous assemblage is reported from the vicinity of the Firth River in north-western Canada, but stratigraphic displacements by frost action in that site are so extreme as to make the apparent associations somewhat suspect.

In summary, the millennium following the disappearance of the Arctic Small Tool tradition in northern Alaska – an event which may have occurred in some locations as early as 1500 bc – is marked by a considerable heterogeneity of local cultures. Most of these cultures show some relationship to the Arctic Small Tool tradition in their stone artifacts, most of them used fibre-tempered pottery apparently derived from Asia, some of them made use of the oil lamp as did contemporary peoples of the Pacific coast of Alaska, and some of them employed large lanceolate projectile points of beautifully chipped stone reminiscent of early artifacts from the heart of North America. Although the various currents can be only imperfectly perceived, this was on the one hand a time evidently without the widespread communications which result in cultural uniformity, yet on the other hand a time in which the presence of certain innovations suggests some active influence from outside areas.

Norton Stage

The Norton stage includes what has in the narrow sense been designated Norton culture both south and north of Bering Strait (at Cape Denbigh, Unalakleet, Nome, Wales, and Cape Krusenstern); the Ugashik Lakes phase of the Ugashik River drainage and phases of the Brooks River cultural period of the Naknek River drainage, both on the Alaska Peninsula; early material from around Platinum on Kuskokwim Bay; early material from Nunivak Island; at least part of the so-called Near Ipiutak at Point Hope; certain of the materials from near Barrow; and some material from the Firth River in extreme north-western Canada.

In the north, it seems reasonable to think that the origins of the Norton stage of the tradition, dating from several centuries before the Christian era, lie in substantial part with the preceding Choris stage, simply on the basis of shared characteristics such as the pottery, use of oil lamps, and the forms of certain implements. In the south, on the other hand, no Choris stage is recognized, and there appears to have been more direct continuity between the Arctic Small Tool tradition and the basic Norton aspect of the Norton tradition. Unfortunately, however, this precise transition is inferred rather than proved; we know little about the period of several centuries which preceded the appearance around 500 bc of the earliest full-blown Norton remains at the site on Cape Denbigh in Norton Bay after which the stage and tradition are named.

In the upper portion of the Naknek drainage, the Arctic Small Tool tradition persisted until at least 1000 bc, when the area was apparently abandoned; the earliest Norton sites here do not pre-date about 400 bc. Despite this hiatus, the forms of some local stone implements of the Arctic Small Tool and succeeding Norton traditions – in particular 69 bipointed endblades and small adze blades – suggest that there was technological continuity. Somewhat farther down the Alaska Penin- sula, the upper Ugashik drainage system has yielded a house with a stone industry apparently transitional between that of the Arctic Small Tool tradition and the Norton tradition. No pottery was found, and even though projectile blades are a clear mixture of Arctic Small Tool and Norton types, there is no reason to suggest physical mixture of two distinct deposits. The radiocarbon evidence indicates a date within the second millennium bc, uncomfortably early for the chronological sequence proposed here. Nevertheless, it is tempting to speculate that the Naknek depopulation followed a contraction in the range of the Alaska Peninsula caribou herd, the movements of which are determined by the constricted geography. If there had been for any reason a shortening of the migratory range of this herd – which today winters in the northern part of the Peninsula near the Naknek River and calves each spring on Unimak Island off the tip of the Peninsula – hunters dependent upon

caribou would undoubtedly have pushed southwards after them. In any event, after the time of the apparently transitional house just referred to, Norton settlement continued to be heavy in the upper Ugashik drainage, with at least seasonal occupation of the river's lower reaches; and by 400 bc Norton folk were also re-established in the Naknek drainage farther north.

On the Bering Sea coast, then, the earliest Norton collections with the full artifact inventory appeared by about 500 bc, while the entire coastal zone from the Alaska Peninsula to the Firth River in Canada was involved by the beginning of the Christian era. Sites are surprisingly homogeneous in major aspects, despite some regional diversity. The dominant pottery is now check-stamped, although linear-stamped ware identical to that of the Choris collections appears from time to time in certain locations. Whereas the fine chipping techniques of the Arctic Small Tool tradition are noticeable in some of the smaller projectile-point forms, in most sites the projectile points have a cruder appearance because of the use of basalt and other relatively coarse volcanic rocks

69 (top row) Norton and Arctic Small Tool traditions: (four at left) projectile endblades of the Arctic Small Tool tradition of the Naknek drainage, south-western Alaska; (four at right) endblades of the Norton tradition from the same vicinity; length of longest Norton blade, 4.8 cm.

70 (bottom row) Norton tradition, Norton stage: two projectile endblades (left) and a sideblade (right) from (centre) the Ugashik River drainage and (left and right) the Naknek River drainage, south-western Alaska; length of right-hand blade, 6.8 cm.

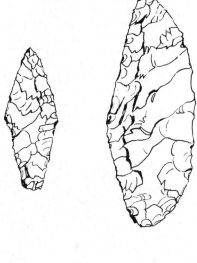

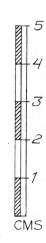

71　Norton tradition, Norton stage: chipped basalt artifacts from the Naknek drainage, south-western Alaska: (left) projectile point; (right) sideblade, to be hafted sidewise in a knife handle or perhaps in the shaft of a spear.

72　Norton tradition, Norton stage: harpoon heads from Nunivak Island. The broad, shallow groove around the caribou antler heads was used to secure the harpoon line and bind the head to a foreshaft from which it would detach itself when lodged within an animal.

CMS

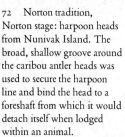

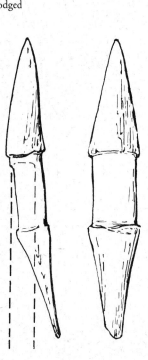

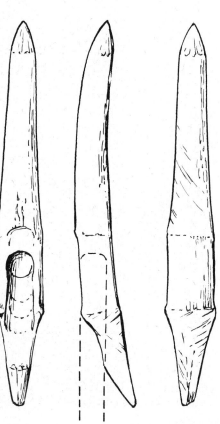

instead of fine cryptocrystalline quartz. Nevertheless, in some southern Norton-stage sites occasional lanceolate projectile blades are strikingly Choris-like. Oil lamps and other vessels of stone are common, and crudely polished slate implements appear fairly consistently, although in certain sites they can be rare. Labrets of coal and bone were now worn as personal adornments.

74

Norton organic materials are unfortunately poorly preserved in many excavated sites. Nonetheless it is clear that a relatively rudimentary toggling harpoon head with open socket was being used in the southern regions, and fragments of a similar weapon occur in the Near Ipiutak collection from Point Hope. Indeed, some of these heads seem less developed than known examples of earlier Arctic Small Tool tradition harpoon heads from Canada. On the other hand, at Point Hope the deposits assigned to Near Ipiutak also include more sophisticated harpoon heads of small size, as well as two large toggling heads with closed sockets presumably intended for whaling. Interestingly, an ice-pick of the sort that came to be installed in the butt of the harpoon shaft for sealing through the ice was reported from Norton deposits at Cape Denbigh.

73

72

South of Bering Strait Norton settlement was particularly intensive, widespread, and durable, lasting around much of the Bering Sea until as late as AD 1000. Attempts to divide collections of this region into

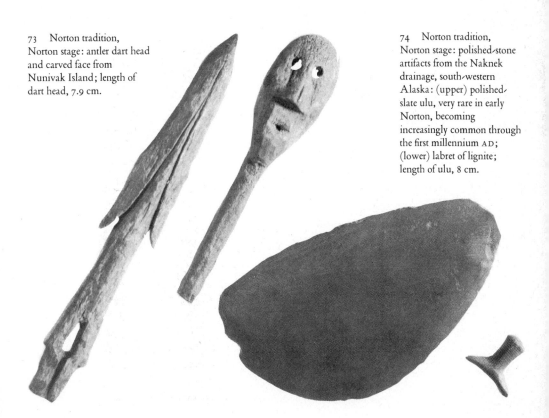

73 Norton tradition, Norton stage: antler dart head and carved face from Nunivak Island; length of dart head, 7.9 cm.

74 Norton tradition, Norton stage: polished-stone artifacts from the Naknek drainage, south-western Alaska: (upper) polished-slate ulu, very rare in early Norton, becoming increasingly common through the first millennium AD; (lower) labret of lignite; length of ulu, 8 cm.

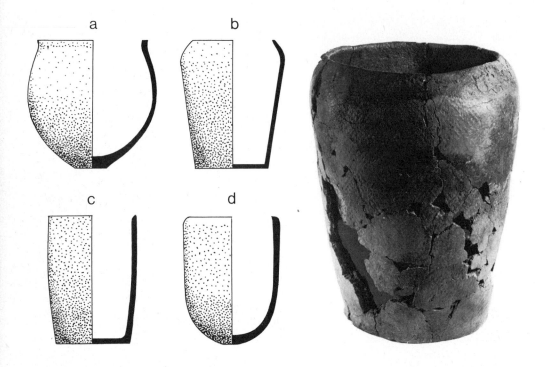

a   b

c   d

75   Norton and early Thule traditions: pottery vessel forms: *a, b*, early Norton tradition; *c*, later Norton tradition of the southern Bering Sea; *d*, Old Bering Sea stage of the Thule tradition. Heights may range from about 18 to about 35 cm.

76   Norton tradition, Norton stage: partially reconstructed check-stamped pot from the Naknek drainage, south-western Alaska; height, 24 cm.

77   Norton tradition, Norton stage: carved ivory paddle for forming pottery, probably of Norton tradition, from Point Hope; length about 23 cm. The elongated check-stamp design that would be produced by one side of the paddle (right) is somewhat more common in most Norton ceramics than is the linear-stamped pattern produced by the other.

sequential phases have been made with materials from sites near Cape Nome, at Unalakleet, on Nunivak Island, at Chagvan Bay, and on the Alaska Peninsula. In general, pottery evolves through the early use of fibre temper to the later use of sand, stone artifacts towards the greater use of polished slate. In the Naknek drainage, where the changes are especially well worked out, the Norton-tradition materials have been divided into three consecutive phases, the first of which is most like Norton cultural assemblages farther north, and the second and third of which manifest local evolution of projectile-point styles, a steady increase in the use of polished slate at the expense of chipped stone, and a shift in the surface decoration of pottery from the use of small to larger check impressions, although fibre temper is predominant throughout. Population is thought to have increased through the three phases.

Permanent dwellings were generally square, excavated up to 50 centimetres into the contemporary surface, with relatively short, sloping entryways – similar in the main to houses of the Arctic Small Tool tradition found on the Alaska Peninsula. The *kazigi* – a combined ceremonial house and men's residence among the later Eskimos – was probably present, a likely example of one having been excavated near Unalakleet, some 8 by 12 metres in size, and dating from somewhere between A D 100 and 400. Its double function is suggested by the large size and the predominantly 'male' cast of the artifacts – projectile points far outnumbered cruder cutting and scraping implements.

With the arrival of the Norton tradition, constructed houses became common on the coast for the first time in Alaska north of the Alaska

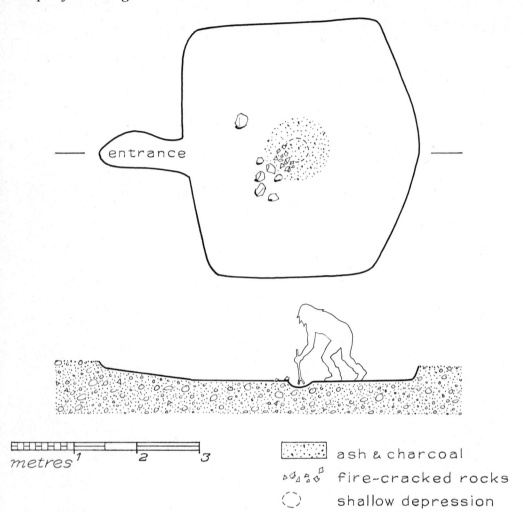

metres

ash & charcoal

fire-cracked rocks

shallow depression

78 Norton tradition: plan and section of a house, upper Naknek drainage, radiocarbon dated to about AD 100. The roof was probably of poles and sod.

Peninsula, suggesting a significantly different subsistence orientation from that of the earlier Arctic Small Tool people. North of Bering Strait, Norton-stage sites apparently do not occur at all in the Brooks Range, but are known in the vicinity of Point Barrow, along the Firth River to the east, and may well occur near the mouth of the Mackenzie River in Canada – that is, in areas which in more recent times have supported a marine-oriented economy. Unfortunately, there is no direct evidence of the use of boats in Norton sites, although considering the near-absence of any organic remains, this is not surprising.

In the south, sites on the Bering Sea coast are often of impressive size – the Norton occupation at Safety Sound near Cape Nome is thought to consist of the major proportion of some 400 house depressions, and that at Unalakleet of most of around 200 depressions. While there is no reason to suppose that a high percentage of these were occupied simultaneously, the number of apparent house ruins does suggest a substantial community. Still farther south, however, around the very shallow waters of Bristol Bay where almost the only sea mammals are harbour seals, large Norton sites are not so plentiful on the coast proper, but tend to occur well up the major salmon streams such as those of the Nushagak, Wood, Kvichak, Naknek, and Ugashik drainage systems. In these sites, notched pebbles generally interpreted as fish-net sinkers are especially common, suggesting that migrating salmon provided a staple resource. In all Norton sites in which organic material is preserved, both inland and on the coast, the use of caribou antler for most of the organic artifacts bespeaks a continued reliance on that animal.

But even in the south, the existence of a strong interest in open-water hunting is indicated by the spread of Norton culture across the mountainous backbone of the Alaska Peninsula to the sea-mammal-rich north Pacific. As indicated in an earlier chapter, this southward expansion apparently started shortly after the beginning of the Christian era; by AD 300, in a site of sea-mammal hunters on Takli Island, Norton-style pottery and a few chipped-stone implements reminiscent of Norton types appear in a collection of otherwise typical Pacific coastal artifacts, hitherto without pottery and with stone artifacts predominantly of polished slate, suggesting that contact had been made with a more northern people. The increase in Norton objects in Pacific coastal sites of the Alaska Peninsula is steady until by AD 800 late Norton influence had all but overwhelmed the local Kodiak tradition. There is said to be evidence of Norton influence also on Chirikof Island, south-west of Kodiak, although we have no proof that pressure from Norton people had yet reached Kodiak Island.

Norton art appears to have been little developed, although judgment is hampered by the paucity of organic artifacts that have survived. Some rather simply engraved antler objects from Battle Rock, near Cape Krusenstern, are thought to be from the early Norton stage, and there are a few rudimentary antler carvings from other sites. A decorated stone vessel, lamp-like in shape but with red ochre in the bowl, is known from the Alaska Peninsula.

79

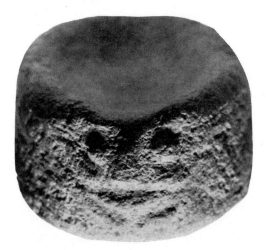

79 Norton tradition: stone vessel from a house of about AD 100 (Ill. 78), Naknek River drainage, Alaska Peninsula; maximum width 11.4 cm. Below the mouth and on each side of the chin appear a pair of bulges representing lateral labrets. Although the form of the vessel is that associated with oil-burning lamps of the period, the interior shows no signs of having been burned, but rather has distinct traces of red ochre, suggesting that the basin was used to mix paint.

Ipiutak Stage

The continuing evolution of the properly Norton version of the Norton tradition was confined to the area south of Bering Strait. Despite an early presence at Cape Krusenstern, Point Hope, and Point Barrow, not long after the beginning of the Christian era these Norton-stage people were superseded by others – perhaps, indeed, by their own descendants – of a somewhat variant culture termed Ipiutak. This particular version of the Norton way of life was to persist in northern locations till as late as A D 800.

The characteristic Ipiutak assemblages lack important Norton diagnostics – namely pottery, ground slate and oil lamps – and their consistently decorated harpoon heads are far more sophisticated than the rather crude examples which can definitely be assigned to Norton complexes. These circumstances might certainly seem ample justification for setting the Ipiutak assemblages completely apart from the other collections attributed to the Norton tradition as a whole (as has been done by many investigators), but for the fact that much of the remainder of Ipiutak material culture is Norton-like. Among stone artifacts in particular, projectile blades, the side-hafted, asymmetrical knives called 'sideblades', and other implements are so obviously Norton that if one were to excavate a typical Norton camp where bone was not preserved, in which pottery was absent as a result of the housewife's good fortune in breaking none, and in which the often-rare ground slate failed to appear, the result would be classifiable as Ipiutak – and, indeed, one such collection in south-western Alaska has been so classed.

In the present view, then, Ipiutak represents a form of developed Norton culture, analogous to the Norton manifestations of the late first millennium A D south of Bering Strait, one that follows the basic Norton subsistence pattern of a relatively balanced harvest from land and sea, with some skill in open-water hunting, but without a great reliance on river fish.

Permanent Ipiutak habitations – square, excavated as much as 50 centimetres into the contemporary surface, with slightly demarcated side entrances – are known from the enormous site at Point Hope, where they number in the hundreds and are scattered along several beach ridges; from Cape Krusenstern, where both square winter houses and smaller summer houses were found; and from Deering on the northern part of the Seward Peninsula, where a presumed kazigi was excavated. Open, temporary camp-sites were also apparently present on the coast in the same area. Inland sites, including both camp-sites and sites with more permanent structures, have been reported but are not plentiful.

Although it was suggested after the original work at Point Hope that the Ipiutak people were primarily hunters of inland caribou and only secondarily interested in coastal resources, the distribution of Ipiutak-related sites which has gradually been revealed seems more in keeping with a subsistence pattern not substantially different from that of the previous Norton stage. The same is true of the portable artifacts. Although the presence of large harpoon heads usually thought to have

80   Norton tradition, Ipiutak stage: two sideblades and a projectile endblade from Point Hope; length of longest blade, 3.8 cm.

81

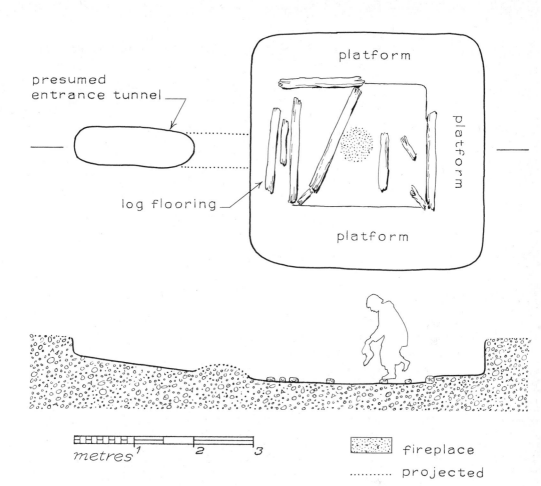

presumed
entrance tunnel

log flooring

platform

platform

platform

platform

metres   1   2   3

░░░░░ fireplace

.... projected

been used for whaling is even less certain than in the Norton period proper, at Point Hope one such implement may relate to Ipiutak deposits. Boat parts were also recovered from these deposits, although none was of a well-developed kayak or umiak form. That coastal hunting was also practised in winter is suggested by pointed objects which may have been ice-picks for use on sealing harpoon butts, and a small hand-drawn sled for transport on the ice. The bone refuse at Point Hope was mainly of seal and walrus, although caribou antler as well as ivory was used for many implements. Refuse at Cape Krusenstern was from seal.

Ipiutak Art
The Ipiutak variant of the Norton tradition is best known for its decorated objects. These include engraved implements of great variety – harpoon heads, antler arrowheads, handles for knives and flint-flakers, and so on – as well as, notably, items without a clear mundane function which were deposited with burials: engraved ornamental bands, openwork carvings, carvings of various swivels and linked chains, animal figures, miniature human masks and larger composite masks of

81   Norton tradition, Ipiutak stage: plan and section of a house, Point Hope. Of the many dwellings excavated at the site, none appeared to have its entrance passage attached directly, but rather house and presumed entrance were separated by an inexplicable low wall of clean gravel. The roof was probably sod. The settlement dates from about AD 200 to 600.

85, 86

84, 83

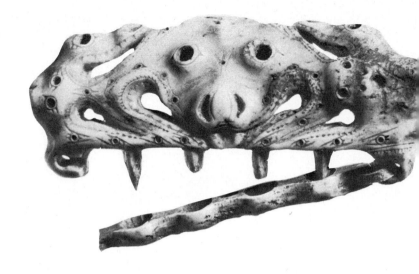

82 Norton tradition, Ipiutak stage: ornamented ivory object, presumably a comb, with form and design elements assignable to the Ipiutak stage, from Point Spencer on Seward Peninsula; incomplete portions of similar items were recovered in excavations of the Ipiutak site at Point Hope; length, 26 cm. Such treatments of the central animal, presumably a bear, and of the subordinate animals that are worked into the design in this way and that, prompted the excavators of Point Hope to stress Scytho-Siberian elements in the Ipiutak art style.

83 Norton tradition, Ipiutak stage: mask-like set of ivory carvings from a burial at Point Hope; height, about 16 cm.

84   Norton tradition,
Ipiutak stage: a bone carving
from northern Alaska
representing a human figure, a
sea otter, or an Ipiutak
shaman doubling as both;
length, 14 cm.

85 Norton tradition, Ipiutak stage: antler arrowhead, slotted to take an endblade such as that shown in Ill. 80; length, 11 cm.

86 Norton tradition, Ipiutak stage: toggling harpoon head of ivory (three views) from Point Hope; length, 8.5 cm. The slots in the sides would receive small sideblades, such as the smaller one in Ill. 80.

ivory, and a number of items in shapes as mysterious as their aboriginal meaning. Some of the animal figures, in particular, were thought by the excavators to resemble the Scytho-Siberian art style of Asia. The discovery of a tiny fragment of smelted iron, presumably derived from trade with Asian people, served to reinforce the possibility of traffic in that direction.

82

THE THULE TRADITION: OLD BERING SEA STAGE

As conceived here, the Thule tradition as a whole includes all the midden-building, polished-slate-making, lamp-burning, kayak- and umiak-paddling Eskimos of later times, who extended from Kodiak Island to Greenland. The tradition evolved, however, in a much more restricted area, in a period which must be confined to the early first millennium A D. It is these beginnings which we shall be concerned with in the remainder of this chapter.

The earliest known manifestations of the tradition derive from St Lawrence and other islands around Bering Strait, and from the adjacent Siberian coast, and may be referred to most simply as Old Bering Sea. Although trade objects assignable to this early stage occasionally appear in contemporary collections from places on the Alaskan mainland – such as Point Hope and, occasionally, around the Bering Sea – no significant Old Bering Sea occupation is known anywhere on the American mainland. The collections upon which the major descriptions have been based were excavated from St Lawrence Island – particularly from the vicinity of Gambell on the west end, and from the site of Kukulik on the north – and from the site of Okvik on one of the two small Punuk Islands immediately east of St Lawrence. Additional assemblages have been found at several locations on the Asian mainland.

Although the various collections are so similar that there is no clearly consistent difference from site to site in major artifacts, the decorative art applied to utilitarian and other objects has made it possible to distinguish two major stylistic groups: Okvik and Old Bering Sea. There are two opposed interpretations of this division: the first, and probably the more common, is that Okvik was the older style, and some proponents of this view have suggested that the style originated several millennia before the beginning of the Christian era. The second view, which is taken here, is that the styles were largely contemporaneous, an interpretation supported by the radiocarbon evidence, the more recent determinations suggesting strongly that none of the remains pre-dates the beginning of the Christian era. In this view, both Okvik and Old Bering Sea developed at the general time when the Ipiutak subtradition flourished on the Alaskan coast north of Bering Strait, and the later aspects of Norton culture persisted in Alaska to the south. Here for simplicity both Okvik and Old Bering Sea will be referred to by the latter name.

In marked contrast to the stone implements of other peoples discussed in this chapter, the Old Bering Sea stone-artifact collections are dominated by polished slate, in forms familiar from virtually all later Eskimo sites, including projectile blades, lanceolate knives, and the transverse-bladed 'woman's knife' or *ulu*. Some chipped-stone projectile *87* blades continue to be employed, as do chipped-stone sideblades used to arm harpoon heads of ivory. Pots are thicker, apparently cruder and generally less well fired than Norton ones. The vessels may sometimes be impressed on the exterior with relatively broad corrugations (broader than the linear impressions of Choris and Norton pottery) or, at least in one Siberian site, with relatively large check impressions (larger than the check-stamping of all but the latest Norton pottery). Early in the Old Bering Sea stage there is apparently a shift from the inclusion of fibre to the inclusion of small gravel as tempering matter, and this gravel temper is characteristic of almost all later Eskimo pottery.

87   Thule tradition, Old Bering Sea stage: ulu in carved ivory handle from the Okvik site, Punuk Islands; length, about 17 cm.

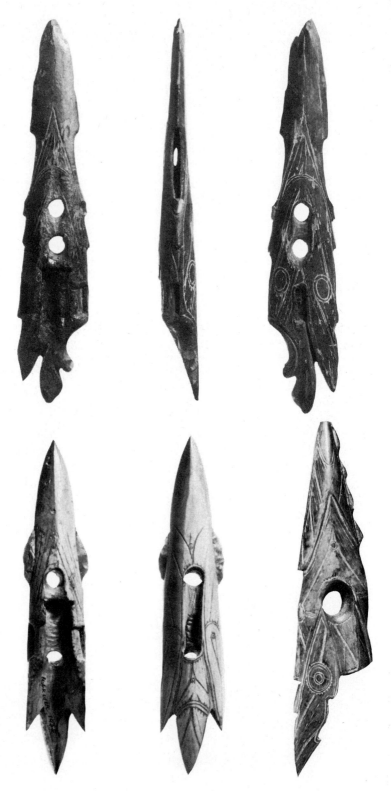

88 Thule tradition, Old
Bering Sea stage: open
socketed ivory toggling
harpoon heads; length of the
longest, 12.3 cm. Slots in the
edge of the upper specimen
(shown in three views) are to
receive chipped sideblades
such as are shown in place in
the specimen lower left (in
two views).

(Opposite)
89 Thule tradition, Old
Bering Sea stage: carved
animal head from the Okvik
site, Punuk Islands; length,
about 7.2 cm.

90 Thule tradition, Old
Bering Sea stage: bone and
antler artifacts from the
Okvik site, Punuk Islands.
Left to right: boat-hook barb,
fishhook barb, slotted-tip
arrowhead, ivory fishline
weight and (right) fishhook;
length of the weight, 10.5 cm.

91 Thule tradition, Old
Bering Sea stage: ivory
winged object in Old Bering
Sea style, purchased at Point
Hope; length, about 20 cm.

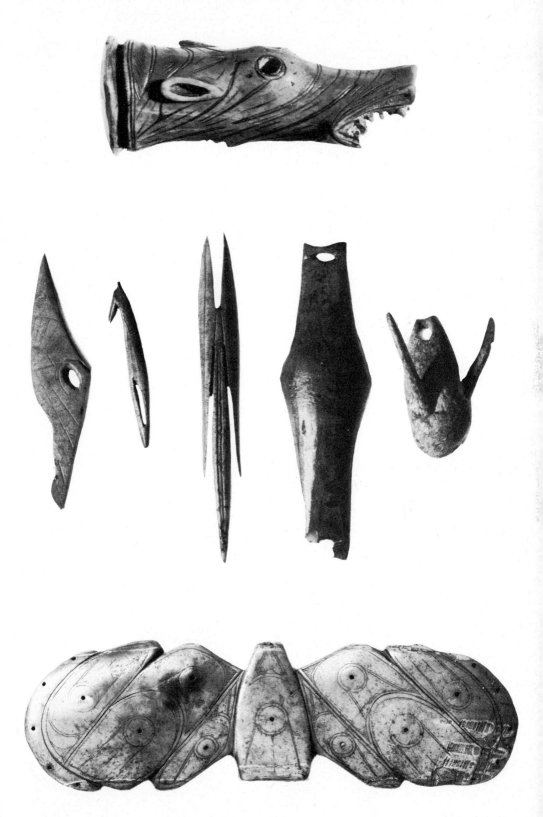

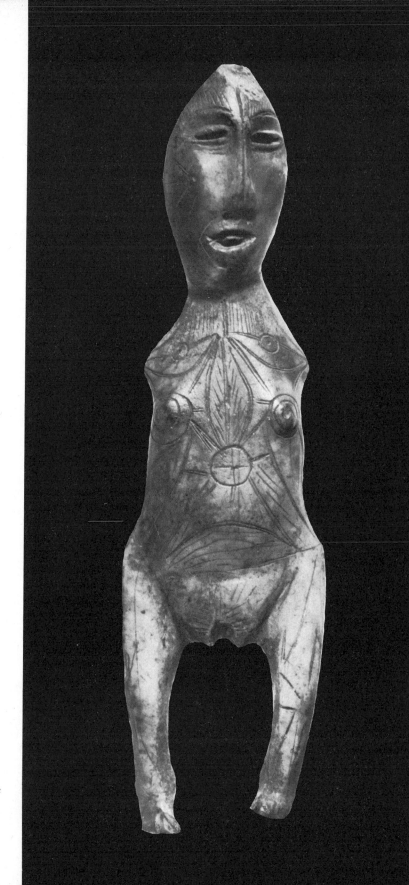

92 Thule tradition, Old
Bering Sea stage: front and
back views of an ivory female
figure from the Punuk
Islands; height, 16 cm.

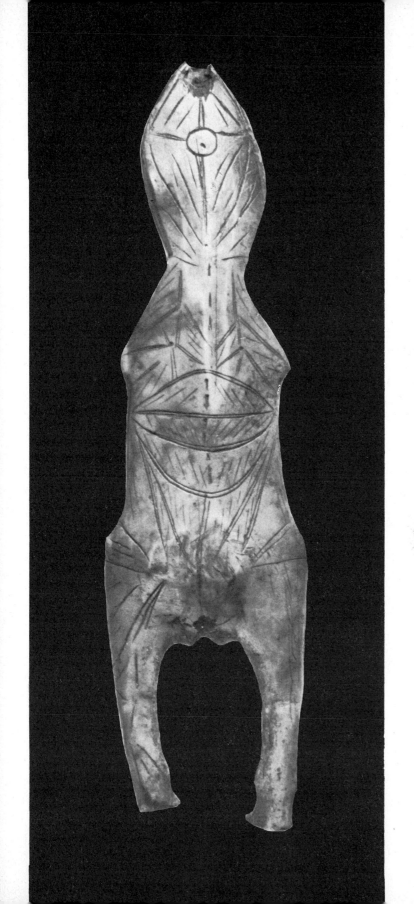

Decorated implements of organic materials include harpoon heads of
88   ivory in varied and apparently functionally sophisticated forms, various
other harpoon parts, snow goggles, and numerous items of undetermined
function. More prosaic artifacts are fat and blubber scrapers, needles,
awls, and mattock heads of bone or antler; seal and walrus shoulder-
blades provided shovels. There is also evidence of some technical
advance in sea-mammal hunting, because float parts – plugs and
mouthpieces – have been found, indicating the use of skin floats attached
to harpoon lines for improved efficiency in the taking of the larger sea
mammals. Ice-picks for the butts of harpoon shafts are plentiful,
suggesting winter sealing through breathing-holes in the ice. Other
projectiles such as bird darts and fish spears are represented, together with
small models of kayaks, and actual parts of kayaks and umiaks. But
although there is some evidence for small sleds, such as would be used
to haul boats across the ice or would be pulled cross-country by one man,
none of the large dogsleds or trappings later associated with dog traction
have been found.

It is not surprising that on St Lawrence and the Punuk Islands people
relied for their subsistence almost entirely upon the sea, but the same is
apparently also true on the Siberian coast, where objects of antler,
although present, are still relatively rare. Most hunting on the islands was
directed towards seal and walrus, with less effort expended on whales.

Excavations on the Asian mainland have yielded impressive burial
sites at Uelen and Ekven, in which some graves have been partially lined
with whalebones. In addition to the numerous decorated objects that
were originally deposited as grave furniture, the presence of whalebone in
such circumstances has suggested to some investigators that those
individuals so buried were captains of whaleboat crews similar to those
known later from the area – crews of large open skin boats, organized
under the patronage of the boat owner. If this was indeed true, it would

93   Thule tradition, Old
Bering Sea stage: plan of a
double grave at Uelen,
Siberia; stones formed one
side, whale ribs the other side
of the burial cavity, which
was about half a metre deep,
floored with wood. Dashed
lines show the fragmentary
skeleton of the lower
individual. Items in silhouette
are grave offerings of harpoon
parts, mattocks, pots, slate
knives and other items.

provide an important new social dimension, as will be shown in the next chapter. Engraving tools with blades of iron indicate trade with other parts of Asia.

Old Bering Sea Art

It was the strong tendency of the Old Bering Sea people to engrave objects of bone and ivory that made possible the discrimination of styles that was mentioned earlier. This has been especially useful with regard to harpoon heads, for although there were changes in the forms of heads through time – such as in the positioning of the line-hole or holes, the location and number of spurs, and so on – most distinctions are based upon the engraved decoration. The decorative styles are curvilinear, including circles and dots and various shorter lines used singly or in groups, sometimes with raised bosses as part of the design. In addition, similar decoration is applied to almost any article that is capable of holding it, including harpoon foreshafts, snow goggles, needle cases, so- 88 called 'winged objects' of uncertain function (possibly used as counter- 91 balancing weights on harpoons), various hooks and toggles and panels, 90 and a number of pieces of unknown function. In the stylistic variant referred to as Okvik, in particular, there are also numerous three- 89 dimensional carvings, many of which represent people. Although some 92 of these items may have been specifically grave art, as much of the art of Ipiutak was, the kinds of objects reported from the Siberian burials do not depart significantly from those recovered in the middens of St Lawrence. Whatever the impulse that led to the decoration of the Old Bering Sea objects, they constitute one of the most impressive bodies of art produced by prehistoric people of the Eskimo zone.

THE ORIGIN OF THE NORTON AND THULE TRADITIONS

As has been shown, by the last centuries before the Christian era people of Norton tradition were spread along virtually the entire Alaskan coast from the Alaska Peninsula in the south-west to the present border of Canada on the north, and had begun to manifest an interest in resources of the sea coast that was significantly greater than that shown by their predecessors of the Arctic Small Tool tradition. Although evidence for continuity between the Arctic Small Tool and Norton traditions has been presented, it would not be accurate to conceive of the Norton tradition as a peculiarly American development, arrived at in isolation from Siberia. For just as it was reasonable to think of the Arctic Small Tool tradition as a localized manifestation of the early Siberian Neolithic, so the Norton tradition shared in similar, broad Siberian developments.

In the valley of the Aldan River, tributary to the Lena, the production of surface decorated pottery is dated as early as about 4000 bc, and appears with unifacial stone artifacts of a late aspect of the Sumnagin culture, which was mentioned in an earlier chapter. Thereafter, both pottery and stone artifacts of the vicinity underwent steady change through the Neolithic – certain aspects of which were referred to in connection with the development of the Arctic Small Tool tradition. By the second millennium bc, the pottery was predominantly check-stamped, and was nearly identical in shape to that of the American Norton tradition; implements of chipped stone included burins and scrapers reminiscent of those of the Arctic Small Tool tradition, as well as chipped sideblades of some shapes familiar from Norton collections. This is not meant to suggest that the Neolithic implements of sites such as Bel'kachi I on the Aldan River comprise what would be recognized either as an Arctic Small Tool or Norton assemblage, but simply to say that many elements are held in common between them.

Although cultural developments in much of the broad area between the Aldan and Bering Strait are either little known or little reported, a related cultural configuration is discernible much closer to Bering Strait, on the Anadyr River. Here, as was mentioned earlier, the third millennium bc had seen the presence of a hunting-and-fishing people who seem to represent a Siberian counterpart of the Arctic Small Tool tradition. By the second millennium bc a Norton-like complex had developed on this base, with pottery, polished adzes and a variety of projectile blades, associated with an economy dependent on river fish, seals and caribou. In addition, scattered finds of ceramics resembling pottery from both Choris and Norton stages of the Norton tradition have been reported elsewhere on the Chukchi peninsula.

Thus it seems reasonable to think of the development of the Norton tradition in its various aspects as having taken place over a broad area that includes both sides of the Bering and Chukchi Seas, an area in which at least intermittent trans-oceanic communication was maintained, and into which some important innovations were introduced from earlier, more widespread patterns of life of the developed Neolithic to the west.

The time of the early Choris form of this tradition apparently was a short period of warmer temperatures that may have coincided with the disappearance of the Arctic Small Tool tradition people from the Canadian Barren Grounds and elsewhere. It was also a period of cultural diversity, and despite the provincial impression created by much of this variety, important innovations of the time suggest wide-flung contacts. The newly introduced pottery was unquestionably Asian in inspiration, whereas clear precedents for the use both of polished slate and of oil lamps appear strongest in the Pacific coastal regions of the Alaska Peninsula and Kodiak Island to the south, while the diagonally chipped lanceolate points that seem to be a part of the overall Choris complex reflect a heritage from the American interior.

By 700 bc, a rather substantial climatic deterioration began which must have endured until about 200 bc. During this period Norton people appeared south of Bering Strait, and by about the end of the period they were found throughout coastal Alaska north of the Pacific.

On the American coast of the Bering Sea an increased interest in littoral resources is shown by the presence of villages probably of significant size along the sea coast, by the initial occupation of insular areas such as Nunivak Island, and by a tendency for Norton influences to creep across the Alaska Peninsula to the sea-mammal grounds of the north Pacific. At the same time, on the salmon-rich southern shore of the Bering Sea major sites were spread along the lower courses of rivers, and in all sites a considerable orientation towards fishing is in evidence. Such organic artifacts as are known suggest that the sea-hunting technology of the last centuries bc was relatively simple.

In the north, not long after the beginning of the Christian era this seaward bent was further emphasized in sites of the Ipiutak variant of the Norton tradition, where sea-hunting implements of some sophistication appear, and where the materials suggest a greater reliance upon sea mammals. There was also an artistic florescence which expressed itself primarily in burial furniture, but also in more mundane items, especially hunting implements.

At about the same time, the earliest known peoples from St Lawrence and other islands in the Bering Strait region developed an even greater, almost total, reliance upon subsistence products of the sea – an occurrence sufficiently important to warrant the recognition of a different tradition, the Thule. This too was accompanied by a flowering of decorative art, applied in large part to objects of the hunt.

The development of this early Thule tradition directly from an aspect of the earlier Norton tradition is impossible to demonstrate with the evidence currently available. Nevertheless, ceramics from the Siberian sites of the Old Bering Sea stage of Thule culture have been thought by some scholars to be very similar to materials from the later aspects of the American Norton tradition. Indeed, if they are related to any other ceramics at all, the widespread presence of Norton-like cultural remains in the Neolithic of Siberia suggests that there is no other possible derivation.

The specific sources of some of the other aspects of the new cultural tradition are uncertain. Some have suggested that the increased use of polished slate and the development of the toggling harpoon depended upon influences from farther south along the Asian coast, although others believe that the maritime developments in the next adjacent region, the sea of Okhotsk, postdate those of the Bering Sea. It has also been argued that these developments and the use of the oil lamp reflect influences from the Alaska Peninsula Pacific coast, where all these traits were present at a significantly earlier date. Yet on the Bering Sea coast of the Peninsula the incidence of polished slate, specifically, during the first millennium A D, is significantly lower than it is in the vicinity of Bering Strait.

The obvious alternative, of course, is that these traits were the product of the particular history of the Bering Sea and Bering Strait peoples themselves. But whatever the pattern of evolution may have been in the Bering Strait region, it was the new stress upon maritime resources, including the hunting of the great whales, that was to lead to the last and most expansive chapter in the prehistory of the Eskimo people.

CHAPTER VII

People of the Northern Coasts

The fundamentally maritime adaptation first displayed in the Old Bering Sea stage of the Thule tradition continued to be improved as the tradition was further developed during the latter half of the first millennium A D.

THE THULE TRADITION: PUNUK-BIRNIRK STAGE

In the period following Old Bering Sea, two cultural variants are distinguished – largely on the basis of harpoon styles and decorative motifs – which are spread broadly around the shores of the Chukchi Sea. More widely spaced geographically than the Old Bering Sea stage, they will be described separately.

94

Punuk

The Punuk stage is mainly confined to the area inhabited by people of the preceding Old Bering Sea stage, and is clearly a direct outgrowth from it. Sites occupied by Punuk people are located on St Lawrence and the Punuk Islands, as well as along the entire east coast and a short distance westwards along the north and south coasts of the Chukchi Peninsula. Scattered artifacts of typical Punuk form or decorated with the Punuk style of engraving have been found more widely.

The forms of implements and the way of life changed only slightly from the earlier period. The wide range of hunting equipment of the earlier stage continued and was expanded, with a variety of toggling harpoon heads, float equipment for harpoon lines, ice-picks for harpoon butts, sealing darts with barbed rather than toggling heads, specialized bird darts, the throwing-board for use with darts, bolas for taking birds, fish spears of multiple forms, the kayak, the umiak, and the small sled. The use of ground slate for stone artifacts continued to increase at the expense of chipped stone, and the use of bone and caribou antler for harpoon heads and other artifacts of organic material increased at the expense of ivory. Pottery was now plain, but still gravel tempered. During the early Punuk period – perhaps around A D 800 – houses were similar to those of the preceding stage, although slightly larger. Later in the period permanent houses on St Lawrence Island assumed the form they were to have until the nineteenth century: semi-subterranean, square to rectangular, with a plank or log floor, walls of driftwood or whale jaws placed upright; two or three large whale jaws as roof beams, the whole covered with turf. Such a house was entered by a long narrow

95, 96

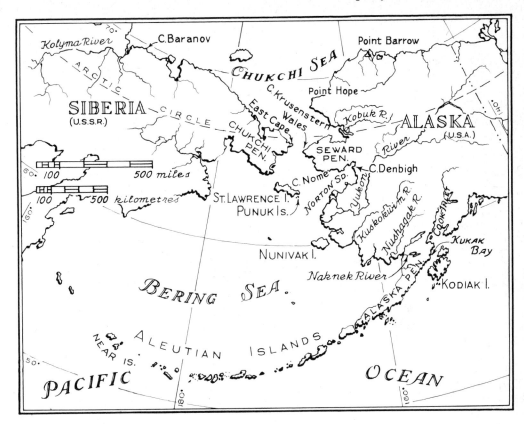

entrance passage, its floor at the same level or lower than that of the house; low sleeping-platforms occupied two or three sides of the room.

Settlements were more numerous and larger than before. Indeed, with the increased importance of whaling, settlements must have grown in size simply because of the requirements of the chase: although there was an advantage for seal hunters to live dispersed along the coastline, whales were hunted at narrow leads in the spring or autumn ice by a crew who manned the open boat, or umiak; really successful whaling might require many more than a single boat's crew. In later times, at least, the whaling-boat owner-captain, or *umialik*, assumed particular importance in the social organization of whaling villages, and occupied a superior socio-economic position. The same situation is presumed to have existed in Punuk whaling villages. That this, or perhaps simply the increased concentration of people, had consequences for inter-village relationships is suggested by the adoption for the first time of armour made of slats of bone, as well as of certain innovations in archery gear such as the wrist guard and the sinew-backed bow, all of which presumably followed Asian prototypes.

Punuk art is not markedly different from that of its predecessors, particularly that aspect designated Okvik, although during the period the customary style becomes more geometric and finally simpler. The elaborate 'winged objects' of the Old Bering Sea stage were reduced in

94 Locations mentioned in relation to the developed Thule tradition in Alaska. Sites of one or another of the aspects of this tradition are known as far west as the mouth of the Kolyma River, and around AD 1000 influences were to penetrate across the Alaska Peninsula to the north Pacific.

97

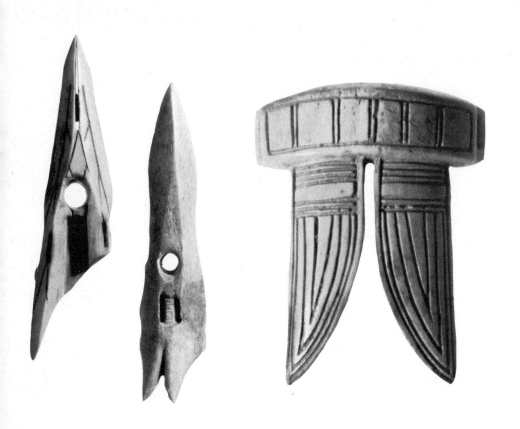

95–98 Thule tradition,
Punuk stage: objects from St
Lawrence Island: (above)
ivory and bone harpoon heads
of characteristic design
(length of longest, 8.7 cm);
ivory wrist-guard in the form
of a stylized walrus face
(height, about 8 cm); (right)
complex trident-form
descendant of the earlier
winged objects from St
Lawrence Island (length, 8.3
cm). Like the winged object,
the trident (or as the present
form is sometimes called, the
'turreted object') is thought to
have been affixed to the butt
of a harpoon that was
launched with a throwing
board.

size and complexity, resulting in the so-called 'trident', which   *98*
presumably filled the same uncertain function.

Birnirk

About AD 500 or 600, the remaining coasts of the Chukchi Sea saw the
development of the Birnirk variant, the southernmost manifestation
having been reported in the vicinity of Cape Nome on the southern coast
of the Seward Peninsula. Although the sites most completely reported
have been on American shores, relatively pure sites apparently occur also
from the vicinity of East Cape in Siberia, westwards along the north
coast of the Chukchi Peninsula as far as Cape Baranov and the mouth of
the Kolyma River. The fact that harpoon heads of characteristic Birnirk
pattern occur in late Old Bering Sea and early Punuk deposits makes a
determination of the exact distribution of true Birnirk occupation
difficult.

The same broad range of hunting equipment was represented as has
been reported for the Punuk aspect. In contrast, though, antler is much
more popular for harpoon heads, which are usually undecorated.   *99*
Indeed, decoration of any kind on anything is rare. Pottery is virtually
identical in clay to Punuk wares, but here generally displays impressions
of concentric circles or spirals on its surface, made with a carved paddle.
An innovation is the built-up sled, with well-turned-up runners and
arched crossbars, such as was later to be used with the well-known
Eskimo dog teams, although whether Birnirk people used the dog in this
way is not known; at least there are no characteristic bone dog-harness
parts, common in later sites. As in the earlier Thule tradition on St
Lawrence Island, oil lamps, generally of baked clay, heated the houses.

The most thoroughly reported site is that of Birnirk itself, located near
Point Barrow. Excavated into the surface of scattered mounds of
midden, the houses were roughly square, 3–4 metres on each side, and
entered by a passageway at or below the level of the floor. Unfortunately,
the inhabitants' practice of thriftily removing most of the driftwood
structural members when houses were abandoned has left us with little

99   Thule tradition, Birnik
stage: bone (above) and ivory
(below) harpoon heads of
characteristic form, Point
Barrow vicinity; length of the
longer, about 13.4 cm.

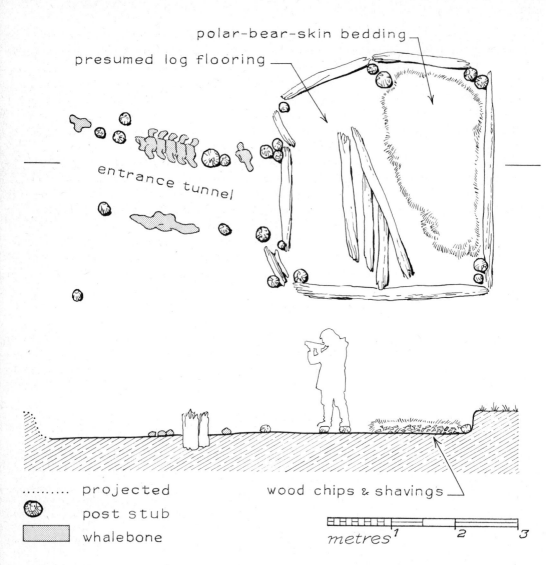

polar-bear-skin bedding

presumed log flooring

entrance tunnel

.... projected

post stub

whalebone

wood chips & shavings

metres 1 2 3

100   Thule tradition, Birnirk stage: plan and section of a house, Birnirk site, near Point Barrow, probably dating from around AD 800. The roof was apparently of driftwood, whalebones and sod.

clue as to the detailed appearance of the buildings. However, we know that floors were commonly of planks, with a platform for sleeping along the rear or one side wall. Wall and roof frames were of driftwood and whalebones, and roofs were covered with sod.

At the Birnirk site, whaling equipment was surprisingly scarce, and for the most part the economy seems to have been based upon the taking of seals, birds, fish, and caribou in roughly equal proportions. Similarly, Birnirk-period sites of Cape Krusenstern yielded no evidence of whale-hunting. Despite the importance of fish and caribou, however, no inland sites of this aspect of the Thule tradition are known, and it appears that the entire population may have been located on the coast.

Although direct artifactual evidence for whaling is poor, the location of sites at whale-rich locations such as Point Hope, the presence at the Birnirk site of at least some whaling gear, the frequency of baleen in constructing a variety of implements, and the quite common use of whalebone in house construction, together indicate that whaling was practised where whales were available.

THULE FLORESCENCE AND EXPANSION

The two or three centuries following the initial occupation of the Birnirk settlement at Point Barrow were a period of relatively stable culture along the American coast of the Chukchi Sea. Houses came to have deeply sunken entrance tunnels well below the level of the floors, which formed a trap for cold air, while in some sites the houses were warmed by a *101* kitchen, set as a separate room off the entrance tunnel or the main living-room, in which wood and sea-mammal fat was burned. At settlements in favourable locations whaling was practised, whereas at others subsistence was focused upon smaller sea mammals, always sup- plemented by a balanced reliance upon caribou and other land mammals, fish, and birds. Nevertheless, during this time there was so far as we know no significant colonization of inland regions.

Although in its broad emphasis the Thule economy appears to resemble that of earlier people of Norton tradition in the north and contemporary people of late Norton tradition around Bering Sea, it seems to differ in one significant respect, and that is in the further elaboration of the range of specialized tools developed for hunting and, indeed, for all tasks. One must presume that the additional labour involved in making these more refined implements was rendered worthwhile by a greater efficiency in hunting. At any rate, that the way of life was successful is indicated by the degree to which it was to expand at the expense of the contemporary Norton and Dorset traditions.

South of Bering Strait, the Thule tradition has been dated by radiocarbon to no later than AD 600, from evidence from Birnirk-style houses at Safety Sound near Cape Nome. By AD 900, houses of developed Thule aspect, containing typical curvilinear stamped pottery and the range of familiar Thule tradition polished-slate and bone implements, were present at Cape Denbigh in Norton Sound, where open-water sealing and fishing apparently provided the staple resources.

By no later than AD 1000, similar houses and artifacts were present on Nunivak Island, and by not later than AD 1100 a developed aspect of the Thule tradition had appeared in the Naknek River region of the Alaska *103* Peninsula, where it is found both at the mouth of the river and well up the drainage system.

From the extremely rapid spread of the distinctive items characteristic of the Thule tradition, it would be tempting to infer that it resulted from a concurrent spread of people, who actually replaced the earlier inhabitants of remnant Norton tradition. Evidence from the Naknek drainage, however, implies that this is not the case. Although there was a drastic shift in the overall appearance of the stone artifact inventories *102* between the end of the Norton and the beginning of the Thule traditions – between about AD 1000 and 1100 polished implements jumped from a

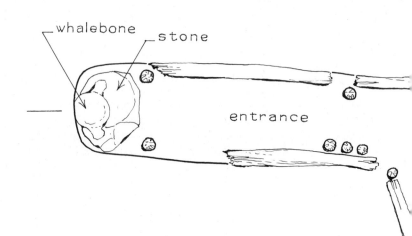

whalebone   stone

entrance

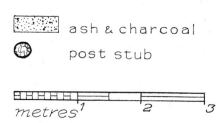

▨ ash & charcoal

⊛ post stub

metres¹   2   3

101   Plan and section of a
fully developed Thule
tradition house, Cape
Krusenstern, Alaska, thought
to date from about AD 1000.
The charcoal-rich annexe
appears to have functioned as
a kitchen. The roof was sod.

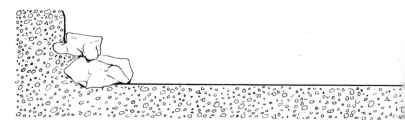

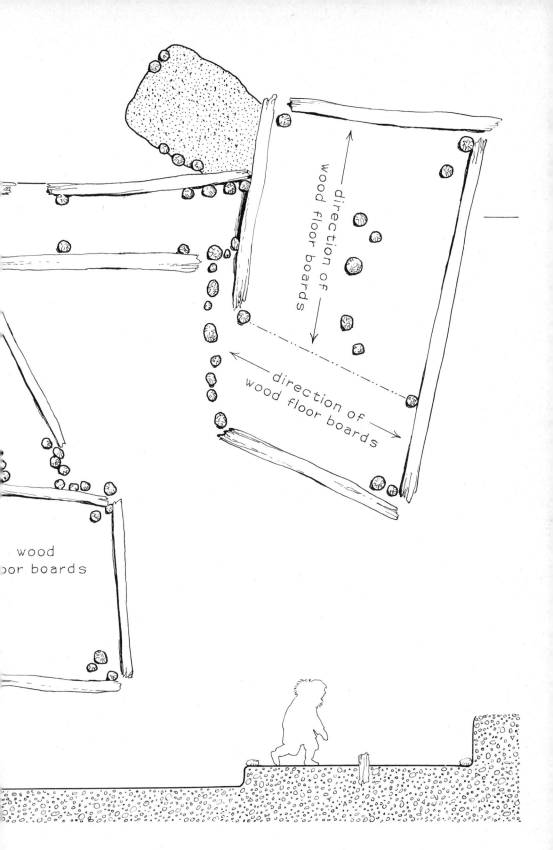

direction of wood floor boards

direction of wood floor boards

wood
oor boards

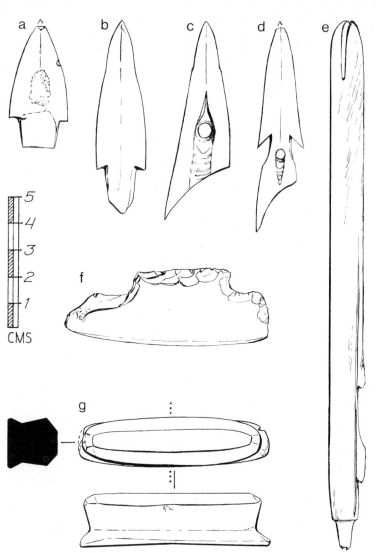

102 Thule tradition: polished-stone, ivory and antler artifacts, mostly from the Naknek drainage, south-western Alaska: *a, b,* projectile blades of polished slate; *c, d,* ivory toggling harpoon heads of unknown Alaskan provenience; *e,* antler dart head, with slot in the tip to receive a polished-slate insert blade (such as *a*); *f,* polished-slate ulu; *g,* labret of coal, to be worn in a mouth-sized slot in the lower lip.

frequency of one out of eight artifacts to one out of every two, for instance – all the significant Thule implement forms were foreshadowed during the time of the late Norton tradition, even if only in small numbers. The pottery also changed radically, from barrel- or cylinder-shaped, fibre-tempered vessels, often bearing large check-stamping on the exterior, to globular, gravel-tempered vessels, a very few of which bear concentric-circle impressions on the outside; yet, during a brief transitional period in the eleventh century, some gravel-tempered vessels appear with large checks stamped on the exterior and others have the cylindrical shape of earlier times. Given this evidence, although it is likely that the Naknek River system received an influx of new people, it is also clear that there was an amalgamation with the earlier tradition and, presumably, with earlier inhabitants.

105

This was not the limit of the southward spread of traces of the Thule tradition. For the only time that we know of in the prehistoric period, pottery and polished-slate implements appeared near the tip of the Alaska Peninsula around or shortly after AD 1000, where in at least one case they are associated with a house with whalebone frame. Although this is probably the southernmost occupation by actual Thule tradition people, polished-slate implements were taken up contemporaneously in the easternmost Aleutian Islands, and their use thereafter spread slowly westwards until finally, perhaps even as late as the Russian period, they came to be employed in the Near Islands at the extreme western end of the island chain.

103   Thule tradition: plan and section of a house of the upper Naknek drainage, south-western Alaska, radiocarbon dated to about AD 1300. The roof was covered with sod.

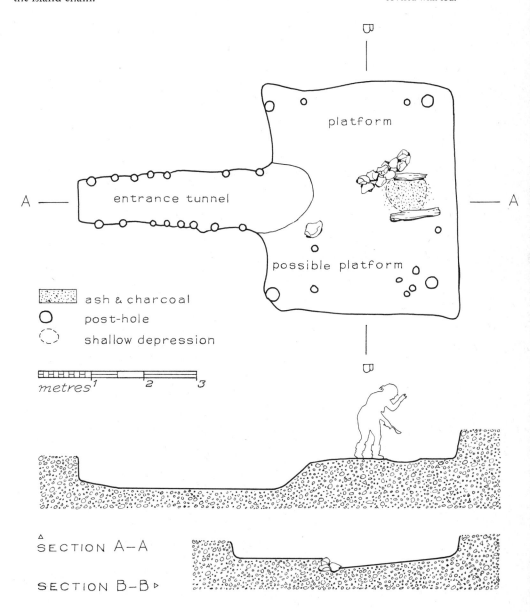

platform

entrance tunnel

A

A

possible platform

ash & charcoal
post-hole
shallow depression

metres

SECTION A–A

SECTION B–B ▷

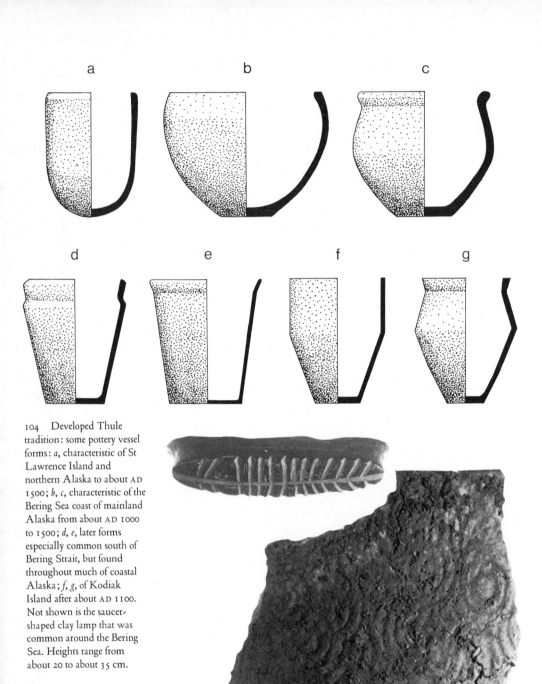

a   b   c

d   e   f   g

104   Developed Thule
tradition: some pottery vessel
forms: *a*, characteristic of St
Lawrence Island and
northern Alaska to about AD
1500; *b*, *c*, characteristic of the
Bering Sea coast of mainland
Alaska from about AD 1000
to 1500; *d*, *e*, later forms
especially common south of
Bering Strait, but found
throughout much of coastal
Alaska; *f*, *g*, of Kodiak
Island after about AD 1100.
Not shown is the saucer-
shaped clay lamp that was
common around the Bering
Sea. Heights range from
about 20 to about 35 cm.

105   Developed Thule
tradition in the west: (above)
coal labret with incised
decoration, width 6.8 cm;
(below) concentric-circle-
stamped potsherd, height 13
cm; both from the Naknek
River drainage, south-western
Alaska, the labret from the
house shown in Ill. 103.

At about the time of the Thule appearance in the Naknek drainage, a similar situation was developing across the Alaska Peninsula at the site on Kukak Bay. As was indicated in an earlier chapter, people carrying a form of the Norton tradition had begun to drift across the Alaska Peninsula to the Pacific coast shortly after the beginning of the Christian era, presumably because of their new interest in hunting sea mammals in open water. Now, however, Thule gravel-tempered pottery, polished-slate implements and houses with sunken entrances replaced those of the earlier Norton-influenced settlement. But, whereas the change from Norton chipped-stone artifacts to those predominantly of polished slate was radical on the Bering Sea coast, the importation of Thule-tradition stone implements to the Pacific coast brought a renewed emphasis on implement forms and techniques long known in that region; for the developing Thule culture of the north, in its increased use of polished implements devoted especially to sea-hunting, had moved ever closer in material culture to that of the earlier people of the Kodiak region. To be sure, there were still unreconciled differences in artifacts between the area of the Bering Sea and northwards on the one hand, and of the Pacific coast on the other – for example, in the more frequent use of the bone toggling harpoon head in the north in place of the barbed, non-toggling head that was favoured in the south – but the overall impression is one of convergence.

Thus it is more difficult to assess the strength of Thule influence on the Pacific, where in only a few sites on the coast of the Alaska Peninsula had Norton influence ever been strong. In other sites, virtually the only conspicuous Thule introduction was the thick, gravel-tempered pottery, which appeared on southern Kodiak Island around AD 1000; but even *104f, g* this was never used in quantity on the northern portion of the same island, although it was in use elsewhere on the Pacific, as, for instance, in some settlements on Cook Inlet.

Partly for this reason, the specific nature of the Thule expansion southwards – that is, the degree to which it involved an actual movement of people, and the degree to which it incorporated earlier, local people and practices – is not sufficiently understood, and is the subject of some dispute among prehistorians. Nevertheless, the clearly increased communication among these ocean-going peoples of the Bering Sea and Pacific must have resulted in a measure of linguistic convergence. Indeed, it is likely that it was at this time that the form of Eskimo speech used in the Kodiak region upon the arrival of the Russians, a dialect closely related to that spoken on the Bering Sea shores, was first adopted in that region – the ultimate southern response to the vitality of the Thule tradition, which produced the people known as Koniag.

Migration to the East

As was intimated earlier, most Alaskan Eskimo whaling has depended upon the interception of migrating whales in narrow leads or channels that open near shore in the spring and autumn pack ice; fleets of umiaks

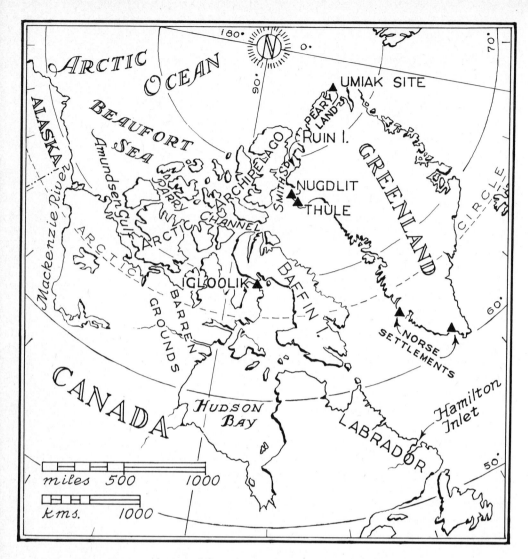

106 Locations mentioned with reference to the Thule tradition in the eastern Arctic. Sites occur through much of the Arctic Archipelago, on both sides of Hudson Bay, on the Labrador coast, in East and West Greenland. A very late movement of Central Eskimos brought Thule descendants into the Barren Grounds.

launched from the ice edge have thus been able to take enough whales to supply the needs of large and stable villages. A significant reduction in the amount of this ice, however, such as may have occurred during the relatively warm period known to have existed during the tenth and eleventh centuries, would permit whales, along with walrus and bearded seal, to move freely over a much wider path in their migrations through the Bering and Chukchi Seas into their summer feeding grounds around the Beaufort Sea and the Arctic islands. It was this, it has been argued, that sometime not long before AD 1000 rendered ice-lead hunting techniques ineffective, induced sea-mammal hunters to adopt techniques more suitable to the pursuit of their prey in the open sea, and then caused them to move eastwards and northwards to practise these techniques on the feeding grounds during the open-water period of summer. Such a technique, in which whales are sighted from shore and pursued in open water by a single umiak and a fleet of kayaks, has been practised in historical times by Eskimos of eastern Canada and Greenland; the capture of but a single whale would be sufficient to provision for an entire winter the number of people required to stalk and kill it using this method.

Whether or not it was precisely this sequence of events which provided the impetus, the tenth century did see the appearance of Thule whalers in the Arctic islands of Canada for the first time.

Although the evidence is still somewhat inconclusive, there is reason to think that the oldest Thule sites in Canada are certain of those around Amundsen Gulf, along Parry Channel and around Smith Sound, precisely the area in which whalebone is the most plentiful in Thule sites. Unfortunately, many of these locations have not been dated directly by radiocarbon. At the eastern end of this channel, the site of Nûgdlît in north-western Greenland can be dated by radiocarbon to the middle of the eleventh century, with some apparently Thule habitations on Ruin Island dating from the tenth century. Altogether this evidence suggests an extremely rapid movement of people in the tenth to eleventh century, along a pathway determined by the availability of large sea mammals, especially the baleen whales.

During the twelfth and thirteenth centuries, Thule sites appear in other zones where whalebone is scarce, these being south of Parry Channel on islands and along the coasts of the central Canadian Arctic, around northern Hudson Bay, on Baffin Island, and on the north coast of Labrador. This implies a slower spread into regions contiguous with the original migratory path, where the familiar balanced subsistence on seals, caribou, and fish could be practised. Expansion did not stop here, however, for Thule people also moved north into the old Independence stage territory of Peary Land in north-eastern Greenland, where an umiak of theirs of around A D 1500 was found. Sometime after this date there was a further expansion south down the Labrador coast to Hamilton Inlet and beyond.

Implements of these new easterners of Thule tradition clearly indicate their western origin. Large whaling harpoon heads and the durable portions of floats used with them, as well as the large open umiak were, of course, indicative of the quest for the largest sea mammals. In addition there was also the extensive tool-kit already mentioned for the western *107, 108* regions: the kayak and various bird and sea-mammal darts impelled from it by means of the throwing-board, sealing harpoons, bows, arrows, bolas weights, and fish spears. The ice-pick attached to the butt of the harpoon shaft now appears with other gear, such as ice scoops and the small three-legged stool, which were to be associated with winter hunting of ringed seals at their breathing-holes kept open through the ice. Also present were the men's and women's knives of polished slate, bone *109* needle cases, combs, snow goggles, and so on. As in the west, decorative elaboration was restricted, and the small carvings of human beings which are found frequently – perhaps children's dolls – were often plain and crude, although impressively carved or engraved objects do occur sporadically. Bits of iron, traded either from Asia or Greenland, also appear occasionally.

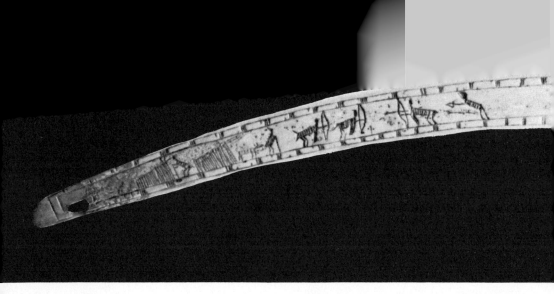

107 Developed Thule tradition or later: ivory drill bow from Baffin Island; total length, 44 cm. Left, a battle apparently takes place before summer tents; right, while people stand before tents, others paddle out in kayaks to intercept a swimming caribou; large boats – umiaks – float upside down along the top edge. Drill bows with representational designs such as this are known sporadically from Canada, and several have come from the vicinity of Bering Strait; they have been considered by some archaeologists to occur only very late in the prehistoric period, but similar designs were present on an ivory bodkin found in a house at Cape Krusenstern (Ill. 101) which must date from many hundreds of years earlier.

108 Developed Thule tradition in the east: harpoon head (length, 16 cm) and arrowhead of bone, and anthropomorphic ivory comb (length, 8.7 cm); all from Cornwallis Island, Arctic Archipelago.

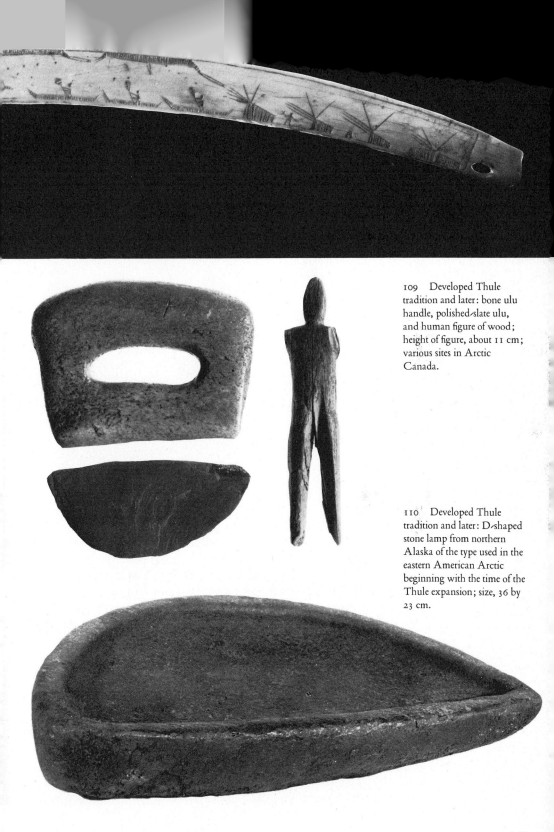

109 Developed Thule
tradition and later: bone ulu
handle, polished-slate ulu,
and human figure of wood;
height of figure, about 11 cm;
various sites in Arctic
Canada.

110 Developed Thule
tradition and later: D-shaped
stone lamp from northern
Alaska of the type used in the
eastern American Arctic
beginning with the time of the
Thule expansion; size, 36 by
23 cm.

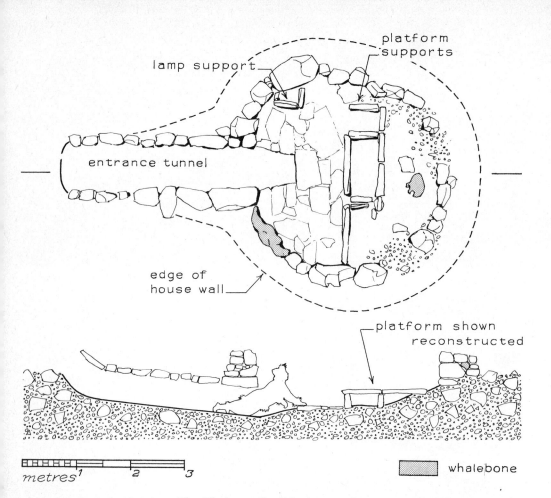

platform
supports

lamp support

entrance tunnel

edge of
house wall

platform shown
reconstructed

metres 1   2   3

whalebone

111

111 Generalized plan of a
Thule winter house in north-
central Canada, drawn from
various descriptions.
Structures such as this of stone
and whalebone, covered with
stones and sod, were in use
after the tenth century, but
were given up by about AD
1500, when the snow block
house was taken up for nearly
all winter living.

110

The Thule people did adapt to their new environment, however.
Rather than the frequently large villages of the west, winter settlements
consisted for the most part of only a few houses – sometimes a single
house – which may often simply indicate the spot at which a whale was
taken by an extended family, making wintering possible. These houses
were sod covered, and along the coast of Amundsen Gulf, where
driftwood was plentiful, they were in the pure western fashion, semi-
subterranean and rectangular, with log floors and sleeping-platforms and
cold-trap entrance tunnels. Farther east, however, houses were less deeply
dug in, usually more or less round, with sleeping-platforms paved with
stone, house walls and the slightly lower entrance tunnels built up of
piled stone slabs as well as whalebones, and roofs framed with whale ribs
and then covered with sod. Although pottery, including possibly the
pottery lamp, was used fairly consistently as far east as the Mackenzie
River mouth, and scattered sherds have been found in various Thule
sites in eastern Canada, pottery vessels were generally replaced by those of
soapstone, and the large crescent-shaped lamp of the same material came
to provide both heat and light in the eastern Thule house. Some use of
the domed snow-block house is probably indicated by the presence of the
bone snow-knife. Above all, the use of a ladder-like sled with narrow

sled shoes, and especially the presence of ivory or bone swivels and buckles for dog harnesses, indicate clearly that the dog has at last entered the scene as the common motive power of the Eskimo sled.

The fate of the earlier people of the eastern American Arctic after the Thule migration is somewhat uncertain. There is no direct evidence of confrontation between Thule and Dorset folk; yet it is clear that in the very long run the particular hunting culture of the Dorset tradition was replaced or else modified beyond recognition by that of their whale-eating, bow-shooting, umiak- and sled-using successors from the west. Some radiocarbon dates for Dorset occupation are as late as the fourteenth century, however, and at Igloolik it has been suggested that the latest Dorset houses, with cold-trap entryway and rear sleeping-platform, betray Thule influence. Dorset contributions to Thule culture exist in the bone snow-knife, related to the use of the domed snow-house which was presumably also borrowed at this time, and in the use of soapstone for lamps and vessels. On present evidence, and considering the very low density of Arctic populations at all times, it seems most reasonable to think that the Dorset people were the victims primarily of a gradual but direct absorption by Thule people, or at least of a steady acculturation to a way of life largely Thule in origin.

When Thule folk arrived in north-western Greenland to supersede the Dorset people there, it was already some years after the initial Norse settlements had been established on the southern part of the island. As was shown in an earlier chapter, Norsemen and Thule Eskimos made contact by about AD 1200 and traded a little in iron and other commodities. These links were to result in the adoption and modification by local Eskimos of some European procedures, such as that of making buckets and other containers of carved wooden staves, but with baleen used for the hoops. The Thule subsistence pattern remained unchanged, however, as did the Thule house – a round, semi-subterranean structure with sunken entrance passage, stone walls and floors, and sometimes – as in some areas of Alaska – with a kitchen in which blubber and driftwood was burned, opening as a separate room off the entrance. This Norse-influenced, Thule-derived culture is termed Inugsuk. And for at least two centuries its people remained in the north, well separated from the Norse in southern Greenland. *112*

By the fourteenth century, a marked cooling of the climate pushed the boundary of the territory attractive to the Inugsuk people southwards, and some of them moved against the Norse settlements. The Norse gradually succumbed, their scattered relics left to turn up in the remains of Eskimo dwellings located around what had once been Norse-controlled fjords in southern Greenland, and Thule expansion was complete.

THE THULE LEGACY

Although all northern Eskimos were forced to respond to the general deterioration of climate that occurred after about AD 1200, the Thule

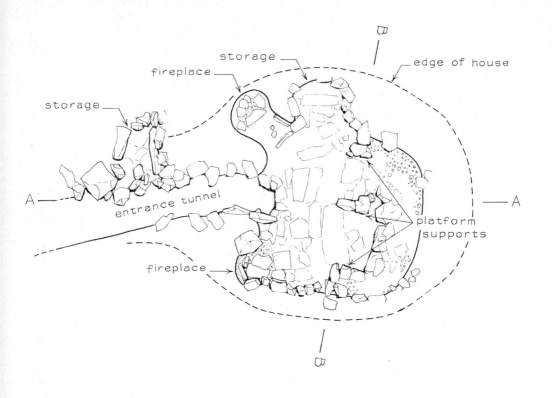

storage

fireplace

storage

edge of house

A —

entrance tunnel

platform supports

fireplace

— A

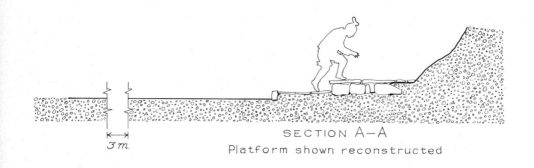

SECTION A–A
Platform shown reconstructed

3 m.

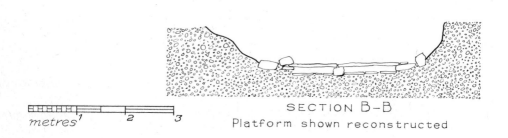

metres 1 2 3

SECTION B–B
Platform shown reconstructed

folk of the central Arctic must have been more hardpressed than most, because the renewed growth of the summer ice pack in the Arctic Ocean had its effect on the migratory patterns of the sea mammals that were their staple. The resilient Eskimo economy, however, with its great capacity for exploiting a variety of land and water resources, ensured ultimate survival. There was a decline in the hunting of whales, as well as changes in the patterns of taking other sea mammals. Indeed, the non-migratory ringed seal, staple of both Dorset and many Thule peoples, must have increased, for this animal dens in areas of new sea ice, and any expansion in the area of such new-frozen ice would have been to its advantage.

By the sixteenth century, the climatic deterioration was extreme. Pack ice advanced into the north Atlantic, where the ocean temperature was as much as 5 degrees Fahrenheit colder than at present, and the disruption of sea-mammal migration by ice must have been radical. In the central Arctic the descendants of the Thule migrants gave up the constructed winter house of stone and earth, moving on to the sea ice to live in domed snow-houses and hunt through the ice for the ringed seal. In summer they returned to land to live in tents and pursue caribou, fish for char, and so to take up a pattern of migratory life almost identical to that of their Dorset forerunners, although their portable artifacts retained a Thule character. Sometime in the nineteenth century certain of these people moved finally into the Barren Grounds west of Hudson Bay, subsisting on caribou and fish the year round, even using their fat for fuel and light, and avoiding the coast almost entirely in a way of life which approached that of the earlier inhabitants of this inland region, people of the Arctic Small Tool tradition.

In more favoured locations, however, Thule life persisted with little change. In southern Greenland the Inugsuk people, once rid of their Norse neighbours, established themselves in the fjords near the perennially open water, living now in large communal houses of stone and earth, and developing great skill in open-water hunting from the kayak. In the north, their contemporaries of the Thule district of north-western Greenland retained a stone house reminiscent of that of their ancestors, continued a life of Arctic hunting, and came to think of themselves as the only people in the world, until in the early nineteenth century they were discovered by Europeans and forcibly disabused of their opinion. On the coasts of Labrador to the west, sea-oriented life including whaling continued almost without change.

In Alaska, the expansion of polar ice created conditions once again favourable for whaling through spring and autumn leads close inshore, and led to the development of great whaling villages at Wales, Point Hope, Point Barrow, and some other fortunately situated locations. Although most Alaskan Eskimos were not directly affected by these localized opportunities for whalers, the Thule way of life in general, with its relatively sedentary settlements, its striking ability to harvest a variety of marine resources coupled with a balanced reliance upon animals and fish of the interior, was successful and was accompanied by an increase of

112 Plan and sections of a Thule tradition house of stone from the central (Disko Bay) zone of western Greenland, estimated to date from no later than the twelfth century AD, a time shortly before significant Norse influence was to become evident in Eskimo settlements of Greenland.

114
116

113

113   Late Thule tradition:
(above left) antler dart head,
length 7.2 cm; (above right)
two views of a small toggling
harpoon head of antler, a
scowling face lightly carved
on the spur (upside down as
the implement is oriented
here); length, 6 cm; both
from an early nineteenth-
century settlement on the
Alaska Peninsula.

114   Late Thule tradition:
whaling harpoon head with
slate blade, from Point Hope,
Alaska; length, 27.5 cm.

115   Late Thule tradition:
miniature head carved on a
small ivory rod, from the
Naknek River drainage,
south-western Alaska,
probably nineteenth century;
length, 6 cm.

116 Late Thule tradition:
walrus man of ivory, collected
at Point Barrow around the
turn of the century; height,
7 cm.

population and an expansion into inland regions. By AD 1200 settlements were established well up the major river valleys – valleys such as those of the Kobuk, the Yukon, the Kuskokwim, the Nushagak, and the Naknek – often beyond the limits of the tundra in regions of forest. Thereafter, expansion into these areas continued, where reliance was primarily upon the products of river and land, although sea-mammal oil for food and lamp fuel was obtained by seasonal trips to the coast to hunt or to trade.

115

Around the Bering Sea in the south, in particular, the rich runs of migrating salmon made possible villages of a size and stability to rival those of the whale hunters of the north. And, farther south still, the plentiful sea mammals of the Pacific coast were hunted by other Thule descendants in a world without winter sea ice, far removed from the realm of the Arctic.

It was with this highly evolved ability to prosper in an often harsh environment that the Eskimo peoples were found when the Europeans began their final, inexorable expansion into the New World in the eighteenth century.

SUMMARY: THE DEVELOPED THULE TRADITION

The Punuk and Birnirk aspects of the Thule tradition, dating from the second half of the first millennium AD, saw maritime hunting techniques from the Bering Strait region transmitted around the coasts of the Chukchi Sea. Towards the end of that millennium there was an even more spectacular expansion of Thule territory, an expansion in two separate directions, both of them probably related to the development of efficient techniques for taking sea mammals in open water. To the south, Thule cultural elements penetrated the Aleutian chain of islands and also reached the Pacific coast around Kodiak Island and Cook Inlet. To the east, probably impelled by changes in sea-mammal migration and feeding patterns resulting from a decrease in the polar ice pack, Thule migrants moved across the breadth of Arctic Canada to Greenland, displacing or absorbing their Dorset predecessors. By about AD 1400, however, deterioration of the northern climate caused further readjustments, forcing the Thule descendants to adapt in differing ways to a number of ecologically varying regions.

And so it was that the relatively diverse peoples of specifically Eskimo speech who were encountered by Europeans between AD 1200 and 1800 all formed part of the great zone of overpowering influence of the Thule tradition.

CHAPTER VIII

Rediscovery : Search for a People's Past

If the relating of varied technological traditions one to another in reconstructions of historical development carries a risk of error, the risk in relating modern ethnic units to archaeological assemblages is vastly greater. Nonetheless, if the histories of modern peoples are to be sought at all, some such attempt is necessary.

PHYSIQUE AND LANGUAGE

Ideally, the ethnic identification of manufacturers of archaeological assemblages is approached by means of all possible data – that furnished by human physical remains and language, for example, as well as by cultural residue. Individuals who share genes form or stem from some social group, and those groups who share diagnostic physical attributes must possess some common ancestor or relative. Similarly, two languages that manifest a so-called genetic relationship will have had a common linguistic ancestor. Given the nature of speech and the way it is learned, the existence of an ancestral language implies the existence of something identifiable as a social group that spoke it. And given the way in which the making of tools is similarly learned from parents and associates, the social group attested either by language or physique, or both, should be represented by a relatively cohesive complex of artifacts.

In practice, unfortunately, the coordinating of information from these various régimes is not always possible. There are, for example, few archaeological instances in which samples of human physical remains are large enough to permit satisfactory judgments of relationship on biological grounds, and the Arctic has provided no exception, despite the often excellent preservation of all sorts of bone. From research reported hitherto in the region, little more can be gleaned than (1) that the skeletons of Arctic Mongoloids, of whom Eskimos and Aleuts are a part, are said to be distinguishable from those of American Indians, (2) that Eskimos and Aleuts are said to be distinguishable from each other in certain cranial features, such as the height of the vault, and (3) that all skeletal materials from the present territories of Eskimos and Aleuts are those of, respectively, Eskimos and Aleuts. Regrettably, precise demonstrations of these statements are most incomplete.

To turn to linguistics is to obtain more information. Several linguists have estimated minimum lengths of time required for various of the component languages of the Eskaleutian linguistic stock to have diverged from one another, and hence from their common ancestral

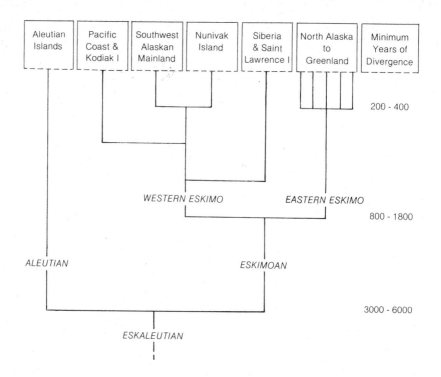

Aleutian Islands	Pacific Coast & Kodiak I	Southwest Alaskan Mainland	Nunivak Island	Siberia & Saint Lawrence I	North Alaska to Greenland	Minimum Years of Divergence

200 - 400

WESTERN ESKIMO   *EASTERN ESKIMO*   800 - 1800

ALEUTIAN   *ESKIMOAN*

3000 - 6000

ESKALEUTIAN

117 Glottochronological estimates of the time involved in the divergence of languages of the Eskaleutian stock. The wide range of figures at each level results from the use of different languages in comparisons and from calculations made by different investigators. Because the maintenance of some contact between fissioning groups will slow the rate at which their speech diverges, estimates are of *minimum* time elapsed; the fit with archaeological evidence is improved if the largest estimates here are increased by about 50 per cent. Years of divergence are indicated as before the present.

language, by the technique of lexicostatistical glottochronology. This technique involves a basic list of 'non-cultural' words (like sky and moon and mother, words all peoples may be expected to have), which is checked for the proportion of cognates remaining between related languages, so that the degree of vocabulary divergence can be calculated and the time involved estimated on the basis of the known speed of divergence of the Indo-European languages. It must be emphasized that estimates of years so obtained cannot be relied upon absolutely, but must be taken only as the most general indication of the span of time since peoples speaking these languages separated.

Regarding the Eskimoan family and the territory of Eskimo speech, a degree of correspondence between linguistic relationships and archae-ological traditions appears at once. Separation between the dialects of the Eastern Eskimo language evidently occurred very late, and it seems reasonable to think that the basis for the overall linguistic similarity in the eastern Arctic region was the Thule migration around AD 1000. The degree of separation between the dialects of Western Eskimo suggests that their formation, and hence the settlement of the Bering Sea by ancestral Western Eskimo-speakers, preceded the time of Thule tradition. The cleavage between Eastern and Western Eskimo, in turn, is such that the establishment of the Norton tradition around the Bering Sea in the first millennium bc seems in good accord. The area yielding artifactual remains assignable to the Norton tradition, however, includes little of the territory that was occupied by speakers of the Pacific dialect of Western Eskimo when Europeans arrived, and it has been suggested here that Western Eskimo speech was imported to the Pacific about the end of the first millennium A D, at the time of increasing northern pressure on the Pacific coast.

As the cultural ancestors of people of the Norton tradition, those of the Arctic Small Tool tradition must have been Eskimoan ancestors in the linguistic sense, from whom also were descended the Dorset people of the eastern Arctic. Unfortunately, direct linguistic evidence for this – that is, direct evidence for the speech affiliation of the Dorset people – was eliminated in the course of the Thule expansion.

Like Eskimoan, the Aleutian linguistic family is believed once to have included divergent dialects, if not languages, which were then confused by the forced movements of native peoples after the advent of the Russians to the islands, so that the precise aboriginal situation is now impossible to ascertain. Archaeologically there may be support for this notion of previous linguistic diversity in the existence of differences between the artifact assemblages of certain of the local areas – especially in the relative uniqueness during much of the Christian era of the material culture of the Near Islands as compared with the rest of the Aleutians.

Still earlier, one would expect to find a uniform archaeological horizon which might indicate the existence of a single Aleutian ancestral group. Unfortunately, times earlier than about 500 bc are as yet known so sketchily in the Aleutian area that the clear recognition of any such horizon is not possible. Nevertheless, the suggestion being made here and based on present information is that cultures of the Ocean Bay tradition of about 4000 bc are most likely to have comprised this uniform horizon. An important implication of this view is that forms of speech descended from the proto-Aleutian language of that time – that is, around 4000 bc – were spoken on the entire Pacific coast from the western tip of the Aleutian Islands to Kodiak Island until about A D 1000, when the latter area was captured culturally and linguistically by Western Eskimo speakers.

To move still earlier, the search for a single complex that may represent the Eskaleut ancestor – the forbear of both the Arctic Small Tool and Ocean Bay traditions – leads us back to an ancient time in which clearly demonstrated continuities appear in neither the Eskimo nor Aleut archaeological records. That ancestral horizon, however, must lie within what is here termed the Palaeo-arctic tradition. Furthermore, the obvious Asian affinities of this tradition and the Arctic Mongoloid physical classification accorded both Eskimos and Aleuts reinforce the proposition, as does the fact that one linguist has suggested that the Siberian language Chukchi is probably as closely related to Eskimo and Aleut as Eskimo and Aleut are to each other. Taken together, this evidence suggests that the early peoples of the Siberian-American Palaeo-arctic tradition included, although they may not have been limited to, speakers of ancestral Eskaleutian and ancestral Chukotan (Chukchi), which are presumed to have been the same language; these people were therefore the ancestors of the most Asiatic of the American natives, the Eskimos and Aleuts of later times. Whether peoples of the Palaeo-arctic tradition also counted among themselves the ancestors of modern American Indians is another question.

ALASKA AND THE FIRST PEOPLING OF AMERICA

If the correspondences just noted are for the moment assumed to be substantially correct, what can be said of the direct forbears of the American Indians? The accumulation of increasingly more evidence from America south of the Arctic makes it more and more certain that the antiquity of man in the New World – the antiquity of American Indians – is significantly greater than the 8000 bc of the Palaeo-arctic tradition, possibly as great as that of the bones of Old Crow Flats (before 20,000 bc). We do not, however, have unambiguous artifactual evidence of this from Alaska. Does this mean that Alaska was not the gateway to America for ancestors of most of the native American population?

The answer of course is that it does not. Given the vast extent of Alaska, the small area within it that has been disturbed by men or erosion, and the almost total immersion of Beringia under seas, it cannot be hoped that our present knowledge includes the complete range of early archaeological remains hidden in the region. Indeed, the number of hitherto unknown complexes discovered recently during surveys for the trans-Alaskan oil pipeline underscores how much remains to be learned.

On the one hand, it is conceivable that the Palaeo-arctic tradition as thus far explored in Alaska represents only a relatively late aspect of a tradition borne by peoples who ultimately were ancestral both to Eskimo-Aleuts and to American Indians. If early American projectiles like the fluted points known nearly 12,000 years ago in inland North America can be shown to have had an Asian origin, and if the similar artifacts from Alaska that were mentioned here in a previous chapter can then be dated early enough, it will be possible to recognize those Palaeo-arctic assemblages containing them as being several millennia older than they now appear, and as representing ancestors of some American Indians. In this case, the progenitors of all New World peoples may lie among bearers of the Palaeo-arctic tradition.

On the other hand, the archaeology and prehistory of Alaska, as it has been organized here, seems more easily reconcilable with the view that the arrival in America of the ancestors of the mass of American Indians occurred earlier than the Wisconsin glacial maximum and earlier than the development of the Palaeo-arctic tradition. According to this perception of the evidence, from Wisconsin times onwards the prehistory of Alaska has been under the control of Arctic Mongoloids, the ancestors of modern Eskimos and Aleuts. Alaskan remains of the earliest American Indians are still unknown or unrecognized.

THE PREHISTORY OF ESKIMOS AND ALEUTS : AN OUTLINE

Although there is reason to think that people have been present in portions of Alaska and adjacent Canada since before 20,000 bc – the

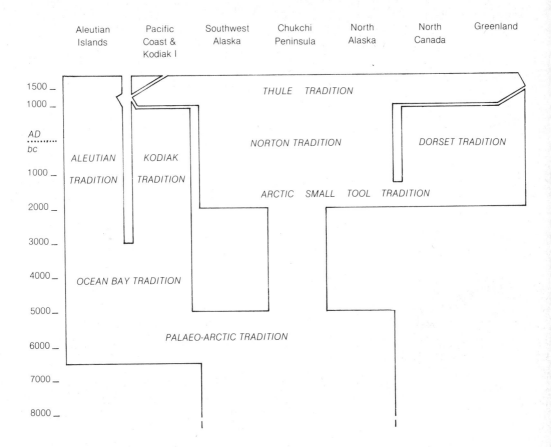

| Aleutian Islands | Pacific Coast & Kodiak I | Southwest Alaska | Chukchi Peninsula | North Alaska | North Canada | Greenland |

THULE TRADITION

ALEUTIAN TRADITION | KODIAK TRADITION

NORTON TRADITION | DORSET TRADITION

ARCTIC SMALL TOOL TRADITION

OCEAN BAY TRADITION

PALAEO-ARCTIC TRADITION

time of the bones of Old Crow Flats – the earliest manifestations which form anything like a coherent cultural whole are those that constitute an archaeological horizon characterized by blades and microblades, dating from about 8000 bc and after, and relating to contemporary archaeological events in Siberia. These manifestations are referred to collectively as the Palaeo-arctic tradition, and represent tundra-dwelling Eskaleut hunters. Their presence in Alaska tends to coincide closely with the zone that was free of ice during the late Pleistocene. By 7000 bc, possibly only shortly after deglaciation of the area, these people had reached the Alaska Peninsula, and by 6000 bc they had been able to move, presumably by boat, as far south-west as Umnak Island in the Aleutians.

By about 4000 bc, changes are evident in two ways: in the interior of Alaska and north-western Canada there is present a set of assemblages characterized by side-notched projectile points, which appear to relate to contemporary and earlier assemblages of continental America to the south. These have been called the Northern Archaic tradition. Whether this tradition was produced by people descended in significant measure from those of the Palaeo-arctic tradition is not certain; the apparent connections to the south seem to imply otherwise. The people involved are here thought to have been predominantly American Indians, forest-dwellers immigrating from the south.

118   Summary diagram of prehistoric Eskimo-Aleut cultural relationships. All traditions that have been described are represented except for the Northern Archaic tradition, which was widespread in Alaska from about 4500 to 2000 bc, and apparently persisted thereafter within the interior of Alaska and Canada. Although it is possible, even likely, that this tradition found some roots within the earlier Palaeo-arctic tradition, it marks a definite divergence from the course taken by later Eskimos and Aleuts.

119 Man and woman
together in a kayak, Nunivak
Island, Alaska; date
unknown.

At the same time, there is unmistakable evidence along the Pacific coast of the Alaska Peninsula, and probably in the eastern Aleutian Islands, for an adaptation to the coast by people now making lanceolate projectile points of chipped stone and using a variety of bone implements, who are here presumed to have descended from bearers of the Palaeo-arctic tradition. These were folk of the Ocean Bay tradition. By about 2500 bc, in turn, their descendants had divided into at least two cultural camps – one, of slate-polishing people of Kodiak Island and its vicinity, producing artifacts in the Kodiak tradition; the other, of stone-chipping people of the Aleutian Islands and the tip of the Alaska Peninsula, bearers of the Aleutian tradition. Both cultures maintained remarkably stable coastal ways of life until the advent of the Russian fur hunters.

By 2000 bc or slightly before, there were present in America bearers of the Arctic Small Tool tradition, descended – probably in Siberia – from Eskaleutian-speaking people of the Siberian aspect of the Palaeo-arctic tradition. Exploiting a tundra environment in which they hunted caribou and musk oxen, these early Eskimoan people spread rapidly from northern Alaska across northern North America to Greenland, and possibly somewhat less rapidly southwards along the Alaskan tundra to the northern part of the Alaska Peninsula. In the eastern Arctic, people of this tradition formed the direct ancestors of those of Dorset tradition, who can be recognized by about 800 bc and who continued a way of life similar to that of their forefathers, but with a slightly stronger emphasis on resources of the frozen coast rather than of the adjacent interior.

In the western Arctic, on the other hand, during the middle of the first millennium bc the Arctic Small Tool tradition evolved into the Norton tradition, in one of a set of related changes taking place in Alaska and eastern Siberia. Oriented more towards the coast than their immediate Alaskan ancestors, now making pottery, burning sea-mammal oil in lamps and polishing some slate, by the Christian era the Eskimoan people of this new tradition were spread throughout the coastal area between the Alaska Peninsula and the mouth of the Mackenzie River. They were especially numerous in the south, where much of their subsistence was based upon migrating salmon, and less numerous in far-northern Alaska, where they relied equally upon products of the land and sea. At Bering Strait and the islands in its vicinity, however, reliance upon sea mammals became absolute almost immediately, and upon this primacy of marine resources was founded the last major change in subsistence orientation of the American Arctic.

By the first centuries of the Christian era there was a cultural florescence among the islanders of Bering Strait, in which the polishing of slate was heavily emphasized at the expense of the chipping of stone, and bone and ivory were converted into a steadily increasing range of implements – elaborately ornamented – for the taking of birds, fish, and above all sea mammals, including the great whales. This was the Old Bering Sea aspect of the Thule tradition, and by the middle of the first millennium A D, a time when various dialects of Alaskan Eskimo were probably little differentiated one from another, elements of this Thule way of life had been diffused around the shores of the Chukchi Sea among people whose descendants would speak the Eastern Eskimo language. By the end of the same millennium aspects of Thule culture were spread also along the American coast of the Bering Sea to the south and had been taken up by Western Eskimo speakers, finally to become visible among Aleuts of the easternmost Aleutian Islands; among the Aleut-related people of Kodiak Island in the Pacific, the Thule impact was great enough for a Bering Sea form of Eskimo to become the dominant language. At about the same time there was a rapid migration of Eastern Eskimo bearers of this same tradition from Alaska across northern Canada to Greenland, as a result of which the Dorset Eskimos vanished as a cultural entity.

With this expansion of Thule cultural elements, people, or both, the foundation was laid for the development of those more recent folk whom Europeans encountered during their own colonization of the Arctic. It was the relatively homogeneous veneer of the Thule way of life which helped conceal many of the varied ancestral threads in the successful evolution of the coastal people of Arctic North America.

Select Bibliography

Two recent works on Eskimo prehistory should be referred to at the outset, otherwise both might be cited for nearly every chapter. The first concerns the prehistory of all Eskimos; the second deals with the archaeology of peoples of the Bering Strait region and the adjacent Bering and Chukchi Seas.

BANDI, HANS-GEORG. *Eskimo Prehistory*, transl. by A. Keep. College, Alaska, and London, 1969.
GIDDINGS, J. L. *Ancient Men of the Arctic.* New York, 1967, London, 1968.

I have referred to the Arctic climate throughout this book. A major source, with references to others, follows.

DEKIN, ALBERT A., Jr. 'Climatic Change and Cultural Change: A Correlative Study from Eastern Arctic Prehistory'. *Polar Notes,* no. 12 (1972), 11–31.

CHAPTER I

European explorations

BANCROFT, HUBERT HOWE. *History of Alaska, 1730-1885.* San Francisco, 1886.
BERKH, VASILI. *Chronological History of the Discovery of the Aleutian Islands,* transl. by Melvin B. Ricks. Cook Inlet Historical Society, Anchorage, 1970.
COLLINSON, RICHARD. *The Three Voyages of Martin Frobisher.* London, 1867.
GAD, FINN. *The History of Greenland,* vol. 1: *From Earliest Times to 1700,* transl. by E. Dupont. London, 1970, Montreal, 1971.
GOLDER, F. A. *Bering's Voyages.* 2 vols. New York, 1922-5.
MASTERSON, JAMES R., and HELEN BROWER. *Bering's Successors 1745-1780.* Seattle, 1948.
MATHIASSEN, THERKEL. 'Report on the Expedition', *Report of the Fifth Thule Expedition 1921-24,* vol. 1, no. 1. Copenhagen, 1946.
MORISON, SAMUEL ELIOT. *The European Discovery of America: The Northern Voyages AD 500-1600.* London and New York, 1971.
OLESON, TRYGGVI J. *Early Voyages and Northern Approaches 1000-1632.* Toronto, 1964.

Native people – general works, language, physique

BIRKET-SMITH, KAJ. *The Eskimos,* revised edn. London, 1959.
DUMOND, DON E. 'On Eskaleutian Linguistics, Archaeology, and Prehistory'. *American Anthropologist,* vol. 67 (1965), 1231-57.
KRAUSE, MICHAEL E. 'Eskimo-Aleut'. *Current Trends in Linguistics,* vol. 10 (1973), 796-902.
LAUGHLIN, WILLIAM S. 'Generic Problems and New Evidence in the Anthropology of the Eskimo-Aleut Stock', and 'Bering Strait to Puget Sound: Dichotomy and Affinity between Eskimo-Aleuts and American Indians', in John M. Campbell (ed.), *Prehistoric Cultural Relations between the Arctic and Temperate Zones of North America,* 100-12, 113-25. Arctic Institute of North America, Technical Paper No. 11. Montreal, 1962.
OSCHINSKY, LAWRENCE. *The Most Ancient Eskimos.* Ottawa, 1964.
OSWALT, WENDELL H. *Alaskan Eskimos.* San Francisco, 1967.

CHAPTER II

Not discussed in the text are two complexes considered early by some scholars. One of these is the British Mountain complex, described by MacNeish from the stratig-raphically untrustworthy Engigstciak site on the Firth River in north-western Canada, where its age was estimated to be between ten and twenty millennia. It was later compared with Alaskan material such as the Kogruk complex of Anaktuvuk Pass, described by Campbell, the Sedna Creek collection of Schlesier, and some finds from the Sagavan-irktok River made by Solecki. Despite the age attributed on typological grounds, geologically pertinent radiocarbon dates at Anaktuvuk Pass seem to indicate that the Kogruk site was covered by glacial ice until about 7,000 years ago. Gordon reports that a site at Trout Lake, about 80 kilometres south-east of Engigstciak, has yielded an undisturbed and buried British Mountain component dated by three radiocarbon determinations at between 2600 and 3500 bc. This last evidence seems by far the strongest available for dating this complex.

A second is the Palisades I complex, a group of crude artifacts found by Giddings on the hill behind Cape Krusenstern, mixed together with implements assigned to the Palisades II complex. Undiscovered else-where, the Palisades I material is here considered to be simply a nondescript part of the Palisades II collection.

Early environment

BRYAN, ALAN L. 'Early Man in America and the Late Pleistocene Chronology of Western Canada and Alaska'. *Current Anthropology*, vol. 10 (1969), 339–65.

BUTZER, KARL W. *Environment and Archaeo-logy*, 2nd edn. Chicago, 1971, London, 1972.

HOPKINS, DAVID M. *The Bering Land Bridge.* Stanford, 1967.

— 'The Palaeogeography and Climatic History of Beringia during Late Cenozoic Time'. *Inter-Nord,* vol. 12 (1970), 121-50.

Early remains in Alaska and north-west Canada

AIGNER, JEAN S. 'The Unifacial, Core and Blade Site on Anangula Island, Aleu-tians'. *Arctic Anthropology*, vol. 7, no. 2 (1970), 59–88.

ALEXANDER, HERBERT L. 'The Association of Aurignacoid Elements with Fluted Point Complexes in North America'. In Scott Raymond and Peter Schledermann (eds.), *International Conference on the Prehistory and Palaeoecology of Western North American Arctic and Subarctic,* 21–32. University of Calgary Archaeological Association, 1974.

ANDERSON, DOUGLAS D. 'A Stone Age Campsite at the Gateway to America'. *Scientific American,* vol. 218, no. 6 (1968), 24–33.

— 'Akmak'. *Acta Arctica,* no. 16 (1970).

— 'Microblade Traditions in Northwes-tern Alaska'. *Arctic Anthropology,* vol. 7, no. 2 (1970), 2–16.

BLACK, ROBERT F. 'Geology and Ancient Aleuts, Amchitka and Umnak Islands'. *Arctic Anthropology,* vol. 11, no. 2 (1974), 126–40.

CAMPBELL, JOHN M. 'The Kogruk complex of Anaktuvuk Pass, Alaska'. *Anthropo-logica,* vol. 3 (1961), 3–20.

DIXON, E. J. 'The Gallagher Flint Station, an Early Man Site on the North Slope, Arctic Alaska, and Its Role in Relation to the Bering Land Bridge'. *Arctic Anthro-pology,* vol. 12, no. 1 (1975), 68–75.

GIDDINGS, J. L. 'Cross-Dating the Archaeo-logy of Northwestern Alaska'. *Science,* vol. 153 (1966), 127–35.

GORDON, B. C. 'Recent Archaeological Investigations on the Arctic Yukon Coast'. In R. A. Smith and J. W. Smith (eds.), *Early Man and Environments in Northwest North America,* 67–86. Un-iversity of Calgary Archaeological As-sociation, 1971.

HADLEIGH WEST, FREDERICK. 'Dating the Denali Complex'. *Arctic Anthropology,* vol. 12, no. 1 (1975), 76–81.

HUMPHREY, ROBERT L., Jr. 'The Prehistory of the Arctic Slope of Alaska : Pleistocene Cultural Relations between Eurasia and North America'. Ph.D. thesis, University of New Mexico, 1970 (University Mic-rofilms, 71–9277).

IRVING, W. N., and C. R. HARINGTON. 'Upper Pleistocene Radiocarbon-Dated Artefacts from the Northern Yukon'. *Science,* vol. 179 (1973), 335–65.

PORTER, STEPHEN C. 'Antiquity of Man at Anaktuvuk Pass, Alaska'. *American Antiquity,* vol. 29 (1964), 493–6.

SOLECKI, RALPH S., BERT SALWEN, and JEROME JACOBSON. 'Archaeological Reconnaissances North of the Brooks Range in Northeastern Alaska'. University of Calgary, Department of Archaeology, *Occasional Papers*, no. 1, 1973.

Comparative material, Asia and North America

ACKERMAN, ROBERT E. 'Post Pleistocene Cultural Adaptations on the Northern Northwest Coast'. In Scott Raymond and Peter Schledermann (eds.), *International Conference on the Prehistory and Palaeoecology of Western North American Arctic and Subarctic*, 1–20. University of Calgary Archaeological Association, 1974.

CHARD, CHESTER S. *Northeast Asia in Prehistory*. Madison, 1974.

COOK, JOHN P. 'Some Microblade Cores from the Western Boreal Forest'. *Arctic Anthropology*, vol. 5, no. 1 (1968), 121–7.

FLADMARK, K. R. 'A Preliminary Report on Lithic Assemblages from the Queen Charlotte Islands, British Columbia'. In R. A. Smith and J. W. Smith (eds.), *Early Man and Environments in Northwest North America*, 117–36. University of Calgary Archaeological Association, 1971.

— 'Radiocarbon Dates from the Queen Charlotte Islands'. *The Midden*, vol. 3, no. 5 (1971), 11–15.

MACNEISH, RICHARD S. 'Investigations in Southwest Yukon: Archaeological Excavation, Comparisons and Speculations'. *Papers of the Robert S. Peabody Foundation for Archaeology*, vol. 6, no. 2 (1964), 201–471.

MITCHELL, DONALD H. 'Microblades: A Long-Standing Gulf of Georgia Tradition'. *American Antiquity*, vol. 33 (1968), 11–15.

NOBLE, WILLIAM C. 'Archaeological Surveys and Sequences in Central District Mackenzie, N.W.T.'. *Arctic Anthropology*, vol. 8, no. 1 (1971), 102–35.

POWERS, WILLIAM ROGER. 'Palaeolithic Man in Northeast Asia'. *Arctic Anthropology*, vol. 10, no. 2 (1973), 1–106.

SANGER, DAVID. 'Prepared Core and Blade Traditions in the Pacific Northwest'.

Arctic Anthropology, vol. 5, no. 1 (1968), 92–120.

CHAPTER III

ACKERMAN, ROBERT E. 'Prehistory in the Kuskokwim-Bristol Bay Region, Southwestern Alaska'. Washington State University, Laboratory of Anthropology, *Report of Investigations*, no. 26 (1964).

ANDERSON, DOUGLAS D. 'A Stone Age Campsite at the Gateway to America'. *Scientific American*, vol. 218, no. 6 (1968), 24–33.

— 'An Archaeological Survey of Noatak Drainage, Alaska'. *Arctic Anthropology*, vol. 9, no. 1 (1972), 66–117.

CAMPBELL, JOHN M. 'The Tuktu Complex of Anaktuvuk Pass'. *Anthropological Papers of the University of Alaska*, vol. 9, no. 2 (1961), 61–80.

DUMOND, DON E. 'Toward a Prehistory of the Na-Dene'. *American Anthropologist*, vol. 71 (1969), 857–63.

HARP, ELMER, Jr. 'The Culture History of the Central Barren Grounds'. In John M. Campbell (ed.), *Prehistoric Cultural Relations Between the Arctic and Temperate Zones of North America*, 69–75. Arctic Institute of North America, Technical Paper, no. 11. Montreal, 1962.

NOBLE, WILLIAM C. 'Archaeological Surveys and Sequences in Central District Mackenzie, N.W.T.'. *Arctic Anthropology*, vol. 8, no. 1 (1971), 102–35.

SKARLAND, IVAR, and C. J. KEIM. 'Archaeological Discoveries on the Denali Highway, Alaska'. *Anthropological Papers of the University of Alaska*, vol. 6, no. 2 (1958), 79–88.

WRIGHT, J. V. 'The Aberdeen Site, Keewatin District, N.W.T.' Archaeological Survey of Canada, *Mercury Series*, no. 2 (1972).

CHAPTER IV

Ocean Bay and Kodiak traditions

CLARK, DONALD W. 'Perspectives in the Prehistory of Kodiak Island, Alaska'. *American Antiquity*, vol. 31 (1966), 356–71.

— 'Koniag Prehistory'. *Tübinger Monographien zur Urgeschichte,* vol. 1. Stuttgart, 1974.

— 'The Earliest Prehistoric Cultures of Kodiak Island, Alaska: 1971 Fieldwork, Preliminary Report'. *Arctic Anthropology,* vol. 11, no. 1 (1974), 41–6.

CLARK, GERALD H. 'Prehistory of the Pacific Coast of the Katmai National Monument, Alaska'. Ph.D. thesis, University of Oregon, 1974 (University Microfilms 74–26, 526).

DE LAGUNA, FREDERICA. *The Archaeology of Cook Inlet, Alaska.* Philadelphia, 1934.

— *The Archaeology of Prince William Sound.* Seattle, 1956.

DUMOND, DON E. 'A Summary of Archaeology in the Katmai Region, Southwestern Alaska'. *University of Oregon Anthropological Papers,* no. 2 (1971).

DUMOND, DON E. and ROBERT L. A. MACE. 'An Archaeological Survey along Knik Arm'. *Anthropological Papers of the University of Alaska,* vol. 14, no. 1 (1968), 1–21.

HEIZER, ROBERT F. 'Archaeology of the Uyak Site, Kodiak Island, Alaska'.University of California, *Anthropological Records,* vol. 17, no. 1 (1956).

LAUGHLIN, WILLIAM S. 'Aleuts: Ecosystem, Holocene History, and Siberian Origin'. *Science,* vol. 189 (1975), 507–15.

WORKMAN, WILLIAM B. 'Archaeological Reconnaissance on Chirikof Island, Kodiak Group: A Preliminary Report'. *Arctic Anthropology,* vol. 3, no. 2 (1966), 185–92.

Aleutian tradition

AIGNER, JEAN S. 'Bone Tools and Decorative Motifs from Chaluka, Umnak Island'. *Arctic Anthropology,* vol. 3, no. 2 (1966), 57–83.

COOK, JOHN P., E. J. DIXON, and C. E. HOLMES. *Archaeological Report, Site 49 Rat 32, Amchitka Island, Alaska.* Las Vegas, 1972.

DENNISTON, GLENDA B. 'Cultural Change at Chaluka, Umnak Island: Stone Artifacts and Features'. *Arctic Anthropology,* vol. 3, no. 2 (1966), 84–124.

— 'Ashishik Point: An Economic Analysis of a Prehistoric Aleutian Community'. Ph.D. thesis, University of Wisconsin, 1972 (University Microfilms 73–09265).

DESAUTELS, R. J., A. J. MCCURDY, J. D. FLYNN, and R. R. ELLIS. *Archaeological Report, Amchitka Island, Alaska 1969–1970.* Costa Mesa, California, 1970.

DUMOND, DON E., LESLIE CONTON and HARVEY M. SHIELDS. 'Eskimos and Aleuts on the Alaska Peninsula: A Reappraisal of Port Moller Affinities'. *Arctic Anthropology,* vol. 12, no. 1 (1975), 49–67.

LAUGHLIN, WILLIAM S. 'Neo-Aleut and Palaeo-Aleut Prehistory'. *Proceedings of the Thirty-Second International Congress of Americanists, Copenhagen, 1956* (1958), 516–30.

LIPPOLD, LOIS K. 'Chaluka: the Economic Base'. *Arctic Anthropology,* vol. 3, no. 2 (1966), 125–31.

MCCARTNEY, ALLEN P. 'Prehistoric Aleut Influence at Port Moller'. *Anthropological Papers of the University of Alaska,* vol. 14, no. 2 (1969), 1–16.

— 'A Proposed Western Aleutian Phase in the Near Islands, Alaska'. *Arctic Anthropology,* vol. 8, no. 2 (1971), 92–142.

— 'Prehistoric Cultural Integration along the Alaska Peninsula'. *Anthropological Papers of the University of Alaska,* vol. 16, no. 1 (1974), 59–84.

OKADA, HIROAKI, and ATSUKO OKADA. 'Preliminary Report of the 1972 Excavations at Port Moller, Alaska'. *Arctic Anthropology,* vol. 11, supplement (1974), 112–24.

SPAULDING, A. C. 'Archaeological Investigation on Agattu, Aleutian Islands'. *Anthropological Papers of the Museum of Anthropology, University of Michigan,* no. 18 (1962).

TURNER, CHRISTY G. II, and JACQUELINE A. TURNER. 'Progress Report on Evolutionary Anthropological Study of Akun Strait District, Eastern Aleutians, Alaska'. *Anthropological Papers of the University of Alaska,* vol. 16, no. 1 (1974), 27–57.

WORKMAN, WILLIAM B. 'Prehistory at Port Moller, Alaska Peninsula, in Light of Fieldwork in 1960'. *Arctic Anthropology,* vol. 3, no. 2 (1966), 132–53.

CHAPTER V

The Arctic Small Tool tradition

ANDERSON, DOUGLAS D. 'A Stone Age Campsite at the Gateway to America'. *Scientific American,* vol. 218, no. 6 (1968), 24–38.

DUMOND, DON E. 'A Summary of Archaeology in the Katmai Region, Southwestern Alaska'. *University of Oregon Anthropological Papers,* no. 2 (1971).

FITZHUGH, WILLIAM W. 'Environmental Archaeology and Cultural Systems in Hamilton Inlet, Labrador'. *Smithsonian Contributions to Anthropology,* no. 16 (1972).

GIDDINGS, J. L. *The Archaeology of Cape Denbigh.* Providence, 1964.

IRVING, WILLIAM N. 'Punyik Point and the Arctic Small Tool Tradition'. Ph.D. thesis, University of Wisconsin, 1964 (University Microfilms 64–10,247).

KNUTH, EIGIL. 'The Ruins of the Musk-Ox Way'. *Folk,* vol. 8–9 (1966/7), 191–220.

— 'Archaeology of the Musk-Ox Way'. *Contributions du Centre d'Études Arctiques et Finno-Scandinaves,* no. 5. Paris, 1967.

LARSEN, HELGE, and MELDGAARD, JØRGEN. 'Palaeo-Eskimo Cultures in Disko Bugt, West Greenland'. *Meddelelser om Grønland,* vol. 161, no. 2 (1958).

MATHIASSEN, THERKEL. 'The Sermermiut Excavations 1955'. *Meddelelser om Grønland,* vol. 161, no. 3 (1958).

MAXWELL, MOREAU S. 'Archaeology of the Lake Harbour District, Baffin Island'. Archaeological Survey of Canada, *Mercury Series,* no. 6 (1973).

— (ed.), *Eastern Arctic Prehistory: Paleoeskimo Problems.* Society for American Archaeology, *Memoir* 31. 1976.

MELDGAARD, JØRGEN. 'Prehistoric Culture Sequences in the Eastern Arctic as Elucidated by Stratified Sites at Igloolik'. In A. F. C. Wallace (ed.), *Selected Papers of the Fifth International Congress of Anthropological and Ethnological Sciences,* (1960), 588–95.

NASH, RONALD J. 'The Arctic Small Tool Tradition in Manitoba'. Department of Anthropology, University of Manitoba, *Occasional Paper,* no. 2 (1969).

TAYLOR, WILLIAM E., Jr. 'The Arnapik and Tyara Sites'. Society for American Archaeology, *Memoir* 22 (1968).

The Dorset tradition

See works by Knuth, Maxwell, Meldgaard and Taylor, cited above.

HARP, ELMER, Jr. 'The Cultural Affinities of the Newfoundland Dorset Eskimo'. *National Museum of Canada Bulletin,* no. 200 (1964).

NASH, RONALD J. 'Dorset Culture in Northeastern Manitoba, Canada'. *Arctic Anthropology,* vol. 9, no. 1 (1972), 10–16.

TAYLOR, WILLIAM E., Jr. 'Found Art – and Frozen'. *Artscanada,* December 1971/January 1972, 32–47.

TAYLOR, WILLIAM E., Jr., and GEORGE SWINTON. 'Prehistoric Dorset Art'. *The Beaver,* Winter 1967, 32–47.

CHAPTER VI

Old Whaling

The longest description is in Giddings' *Ancient Men of the Arctic.* It is difficult to reconcile his 1700 bc dating of Old Whaling, which follows manifestations of the Arctic Small Tool tradition at Cape Krusenstern, with the growing body of evidence indicating that people of the Arctic Small Tool tradition were scarcely present in Alaska before 2000 bc. The discrepancy might be explained if the Old Whaling radiocarbon determinations were on either sea-mammal fat or fat-impregnated wood; blubber is now suspected of yielding dates substantially older than those obtained from clean wood charcoal.

The Norton tradition (all aspects)

BOCKSTOCE, JOHN. 'A Prehistoric Population Change in the Bering Strait Region'. *Polar Record,* vol. 16 (1973), 793–803.

DUMOND, DON E. 'On the Presumed Spread of Slate Grinding in Alaska'. *Arctic Anthropology,* vol. 5, no. 1 (1968), 82–91.

— 'A Summary of Archaeology in the Katmai Region, Southwestern Alaska'. *University of Oregon Anthropological Papers,* no. 2 (1971).

GIDDINGS, J. L. 'Round Houses in the Western Arctic'. *American Antiquity,* vol. 23 (1957), 121–35.

— 'Cultural Continuities of Eskimos'. *American Antiquity,* vol. 27 (1961), 155–73.

— 'Some Arctic Spear Points and Their Counterparts'. *Anthropological Papers of the University of Alaska,* vol. 10, no. 2 (1963), 1–12.

LARSEN, HELGE. 'Archaeological Investigations in Southwestern Alaska'. *American Antiquity,* vol. 15 (1950), 122–86.

— 'Trail Creek'. *Acta Arctica,* no. 15 (1968).

LARSEN, HELGE, and FROELICH RAINEY. 'Ipiutak and the Arctic Whale Hunting Culture'. *Anthropological Papers of the American Museum of Natural History,* vol. 42 (1948).

LUTZ, BRUCE J. 'A Methodology for Determining Regional Intra-Cultural Variation within Norton, an Alaskan Archaeological Culture'. Ph.D. thesis, University of Pennsylvania, 1972 (University Microfilms 72–25,624).

— 'An Archaeological *Karigi* at the Site of UngaLaqLiq, Western Alaska'. *Arctic Anthropology,* vol. 10, no. 1 (1973), 111–18.

NOWAK, MICHAEL. 'A Preliminary Report on the Archaeology of Nunivak Island, Alaska'. *Anthropological Papers of the University of Alaska,* vol. 15, no. 1 (1971), 18–31.

ROSS, RICHARD E. 'The Cultural Sequence at Chagvan Bay, Alaska: A Matrix Analysis'. Ph.D. thesis, Washington State University, 1971 (University Microfilms 72–7680).

The Thule tradition: Old Bering Sea stage

COLLINS, H. B., Jr. 'Archaeology of St Lawrence Island, Alaska'. *Smithsonian Miscellaneous Collections,* vol. 96, no. 1 (1937).

GEIST, OTTO W., and F. G. RAINEY. 'Archaeological Excavations at Kukulik, St Lawrence Island, Alaska. *Miscellaneous Publications of the University of Alaska,* no. 2 (1936).

RAINEY, FROELICH G. 'Eskimo Prehistory: The Okvik Site on the Punuk Islands'. *Anthropological Papers of the American Museum of Natural History,* vol. 37, no. 4 (1941), 443–569.

RUDENKO, S. I. 'The Ancient Culture of the Bering Sea and the Eskimo Problem', transl. by Paul Tolstoy. Arctic Institute of North America, Anthropology of the North, *Translations from Russian Sources,* no. 1. Toronto, 1961.

Origin of traditions

CHARD, CHESTER S. *Northeast Asia in Prehistory.* Madison, 1974.

DIKOV, N. N. 'The Stone Age of Kamchatka and the Chukchi Peninsula in the Light of New Archaeological Data'. *Arctic Anthropology,* vol. 3, no. 1 (1965), 10–25.

DUMOND, DON E. 'The Prehistoric Pottery of Southwestern Alaska'. *Anthropological Papers of the University of Alaska,* vol. 14, no. 2 (1969), 18–42.

GRIFFIN, JAMES B. 'Northeast Asian and Northwestern American Ceramics'. *Proceedings of the VIIIth International Congress of Anthropological and Ethnological Sciences, Tokyo and Kyoto, 1968,* vol. 3 (1970), 327–30.

LARSEN, HELGE. 'Near Ipiutak and Uwelen-Okvik'. *Folk,* vol. 10 (1968), 81–90.

CHAPTER VII

The Thule tradition: Punuk-Birnirk stage

COLLINS, H. B., Jr. 'Archaeology of St Lawrence Island, Alaska'. *Smithsonian Miscellaneous Collections,* vol. 96, no. 1 (1937).

FORD, JAMES A. 'Eskimo Prehistory in the Vicinity of Point Barrow, Alaska'. *Anthropological Papers of the American Museum of Natural History,* vol. 47, pt. 1 (1959).

GEIST, OTTO W., and F. G. RAINEY. 'Archaeological Excavations at Kukulik, St Lawrence Island, Alaska'. *Miscellaneous Publications of the University of Alaska,* no. 2 (1936).

RUDENKO, S. I. 'The Ancient Culture of the Bering Sea and the Eskimo Problem', transl. by Paul Tolstoy. Arctic Institute of

North America, Anthropology of the North, *Translations from Russian Sources,* no. 1. Toronto, 1961.

STANFORD, DENNIS J. 'The Origin of Thule Culture'. Ph.D. thesis, University of New Mexico, 1972 (University Microfilms 73–27813).

The Thule tradition – development, expansion, legacy

Stanford, cited above and below, gives a somewhat different interpretation of Thule development and of the Thule movement across Arctic Canada than that adopted here.

CLARK, DONALD W. 'Koniag Prehistory'. *Tübinger Monographien zur Urgeschichte,* vol. 1. Stuttgart, 1974.

DUMOND, DON E. 'Prehistoric Cultural Contacts in Southwestern Alaska'. *Science,* vol. 166 (1969), 1108–15.

— 'The Prehistoric Pottery of Southwestern Alaska'. *Anthropological Papers of the University of Alaska,* vol. 14, no. 2 (1969), 18–42.

— 'A Summary of Archaeology in the Katmai Region, Southwestern Alaska'. *University of Oregon Anthropological Papers,* no. 2 (1971).

DUMOND, DON E., and ROBERT L. A. MACE. 'An Archaeological Survey along Knik Arm'. *Anthropological Papers of the University of Alaska,* vol. 14, no. 1 (1968), 1–21.

FITZHUGH, WILLIAM W. 'Environmental Archaeology and Cultural Systems in Hamilton Inlet, Labrador'. *Smithsonian Contributions to Anthropology,* no. 16 (1972).

GAD, FINN. *The History of Greenland,* vol. 1: *From Earliest Times to 1700,* transl. by E. Dupont. London, 1970, Montreal, 1971. (Contains summaries of work by Holtved, Mathiassen, and others, with source citations.)

GIDDINGS, J. L. 'The Arctic Woodland Culture of the Kobuk River'. University of Pennsylvania, *Museum Monographs.* 1952.

— *The Archaeology of Cape Denbigh.* Providence, 1964.

MCCARTNEY, A. P. 'Prehistoric Cultural Integration along the Alaska Peninsula'. *Anthropological Papers of the University of Alaska,* vol. 16, no. 1 (1974), 59–84.

MCGHEE, ROBERT. 'Speculations on Climatic Change and Thule Culture Development'. *Folk,* vol. 11/12 (1969/70), 173–84.

— 'Copper Eskimo Prehistory'. National Museums of Canada, *Publications in Archaeology,* no. 2 (1972).

MATHIASSEN, THERKEL. 'Archaeology of the Central Eskimos'. *Report of the Fifth Thule Expedition 1921–1924,* vol. 4. Copenhagen, 1927.

NOWAK, MICHAEL. 'A Preliminary Report on the Archaeology of Nunivak Island, Alaska'. *Anthropological Papers of the University of Alaska,* vol. 15, no. 1 (1971), 18–31.

STANFORD, DENNIS J. 'The Origin of Thule Culture'. Ph.D. thesis, University of New Mexico, 1972 (University Microfilms 73–27813).

TURNER, CHRISTY G. II, and JACQUELINE A. TURNER. 'Progress Report on Evolutionary Anthropological Study of Akun Strait District, Eastern Aleutians, Alaska'. *Anthropological Papers of the University of Alaska,* vol. 16, no. 1 (1974), 27–57.

CHAPTER VIII

Except for those few scholars who will not hazard any ethnic attributions at all to archaeological remains older than the latest prehistoric period, there is reasonable agreement among Arctic archaeologists regarding the general outlines of the reconstruction of Eskaleut prehistory as given here. In fairness, certain areas where major disagreements do exist should be mentioned.

There is definite argument over whether the Anangula complex of 6000 bc should be included with other American examples of what is here called the Siberian-American Palaeo-arctic tradition, or whether it should be classed by itself. There is a notable lack of agreement over whether the Aleutian tradition, surely recognizable after 2500 bc, really developed from the Anangula complex.

There is considerable skepticism regarding the presence of the Ocean Bay tradition in the eastern Aleutian Islands, and hence regarding the possibility of the development of that tradition from something like the Anangula complex, and therefore the possibility of certain continuities between the Palaeo-arctic tradition, the Ocean Bay tradition and the Aleutian and Kodiak traditions. All these concern the southern Bering Sea and the Pacific regions, all are crucial to the fundamental relationship between Eskimos and Aleuts, and all of them have been touched on at least to some extent in this book.

In addition, there remains some question concerning the location in which the Arctic Small Tool tradition evolved from the earlier Palaeo-arctic tradition, although there seems to be agreement that such an evolution did occur. Some feel that the development took place in America, even though the American record grows clearer every year and provides no clear evidence of it. Neither is there direct evidence that the evolution occurred in Asia, although the lacunae in the Siberian archaeological record are great enough that on the basis of information now at hand it appears much easier to propose that location.

The following relate to one or more of these questions.

AIGNER, JEAN S. 'Studies in the Early Prehistory of Nikolski Bay: 1937–1971'. *Anthropological Papers of the University of Alaska,* vol. 16, no. 1 (1974), 9–25.

CLARK, DONALD W. 'The Earliest Prehistoric Cultures of Kodiak Island, Alaska: 1971 Field Work, Preliminary Report'. *Arctic Anthropology,* vol. 11, no. 1 (1974), 41–6.

DUMOND, DON E. 'Eskimos and Aleuts'. *Proceedings of the VIIIth International Congress of Anthropological and Ethnological Sciences, Tokyo and Kyoto, 1968,* vol. 3 (1970), 102–7.

IRVING, W. N. 'The Arctic Small Tool Tradition'. *Proceedings of the VIIIth International Congress of Anthropological and Ethnological Sciences, Tokyo and Kyoto, 1968,* vol. 3 (1970), 340–2.

LAUGHLIN, WILLIAM S. 'Aleuts: Ecosystem, Holocene History, and Siberian Origin'. *Science,* vol. 189 (1975), 507–15.

MCCARTNEY, A. P. 'A Proposed Western Aleutian Phase in the Near Islands, Alaska'. *Arctic Anthropology,* vol. 8, no. 2 (1971), 92–142.

List of Illustrations

The author and publishers are grateful to the persons and institutions listed below who have made photographs available and/or provided permission to publish them. Where not otherwise indicated, photographs are by the author, and specimens shown are in the Oregon State Museum of Anthropology, a division of the University of Oregon Museum of Natural History.

All line illustrations were drawn by Carol Steichen Dumond. Sources consulted and repositories of artifacts other than those in the Oregon State Museum of Anthropology are given below.

Index

Index